Music in Turkey

Music in Turkey

EXPERIENCING MUSIC,
EXPRESSING CULTURE

ELIOT BATES

New York   Oxford
OXFORD UNIVERSITY PRESS
2011

Oxford University Press, Inc., publishes works that further Oxford University's
objective of excellence in research, scholarship, and education.

Oxford   New York
Auckland   Cape Town   Dar es Salaam   Hong Kong   Karachi
Kuala Lumpur   Madrid   Melbourne   Mexico City   Nairobi
New Delhi   Shanghai   Taipei   Toronto

With offices in
Argentina   Austria   Brazil   Chile   Czech Republic   France   Greece
Guatemala   Hungary   Italy   Japan   Poland   Portugal   Singapore
South Korea   Switzerland   Thailand   Turkey   Ukraine   Vietnam

Copyright © 2011 by Oxford University Press, Inc.

Published by Oxford University Press, Inc.
198 Madison Avenue, New York, New York 10016
http://www.oup.com

Library of Congress Cataloging-in-Publication Data

Bates, Eliot.
Music in Turkey : experiencing music, expressing culture / Eliot Bates.
    p. cm.—(Global music series)
Includes bibliographical references and index.
ISBN 978-0-19-539414-6 (pbk. (main))—ISBN 978-0-19-539415-3 (hardback)
1. Music—Turkey—History and criticism. 2. Music—Social aspects—Turkey.
3. Ethnomusicology. I. Title.
ML345.T8B37   2011
780.9561—dc22   2010009178

Printing number: 9 8 7 6 5 4 3 2 1

Printed in the United States of America
on acid-free paper

Contents

5. Music, Politics, and Meaning   99

Foreword

∞

In the past three decades interest in music around the world has surged, as evidenced in the proliferation of courses at the college level, the burgeoning "world music" market in the recording business, and the extent to which musical performance is evoked as a lure in the international tourist industry. This has encouraged an explosion in ethnomusicological research and publication including production of reference works and textbooks. The original model for the "world music" course—if this is Tuesday, this must be Japan—has grown old as has the format of textbooks for it, either a series of articles in single multi-authored volumes that subscribe to the idea of "a survey" and have created a canon of cultures for study, or single-authored studies purporting to cover world musics or ethnomusicology. The time has come for a change.

This Global Music Series offers a new paradigm. Instructors can now design their own courses; choosing from a set of case study volumes, they can decide which and how much music they will teach. The Series also does something else; rather than uniformly taking a large region and giving superficial examples from several different countries within it, case studies offer two formats—some focused on a specific culture, some on a discrete geographical area. In either case, each volume offers greater depth than the usual survey. Themes significant in each instance guide the choice of music that is discussed. The contemporary musical situation is the point of departure in all the volumes, with historical information and traditions covered as they elucidate the present. In addition, a set of unifying topics such as gender, globalization, and authenticity occur throughout the series. These are addressed in the framing volume, *Thinking Musically* (Wade), which sets the stage for the case studies by introducing those topics and other ways to think about how people make music meaningful and useful in their lives. *Thinking Musically* also presents the basic elements of music as they are practiced in musical systems around the world so that authors of each case study do not have to spend time explaining them and can delve immediately into the particular music. A second framing volume, *Teaching Music*

Globally (Campbell), guides teachers in the use of *Thinking Musically* and the case studies.

The series sub-title, "Experiencing Music, Expressing Culture," also puts in the forefront the people who make music or in some other way experience it and also through it express shared culture. This resonance with global studies in such disciplines as history and anthropology, with their focus on processes and themes that permit cross-study, occasions the title of this Global Music Series.

Bonnie C. Wade
Patricia Shehan Campbell
General Editors

Preface

∽

My aim in writing this book is to introduce music in contemporary Turkey to a general readership, including students and teachers of ethnomusicology, and readers interested in learning about contemporary expressive arts in West Asia. My primary focus is on music in present-day Istanbul, including musics brought by migrants from rural Anatolia to Istanbul (Chapter 1), urban art and folk musics (Chapter 2), contemporary arrangements of urban and rural music (Chapter 4), and musics with political meanings (Chapter 5).

Four interrelated themes recur throughout this book and connect the listening examples, activities, visuals, and text. The first theme: music in Turkey has been, and continues to be, an integral part of national identity and the formation of a national consciousness about local and regional cultural differences, resulting in a multiplicity of meanings of those musics in modern Turkey. Second: numerous technologies play a central role in the creation of new interpretations of traditional and art musics in Turkey (a process known as arrangement). Third: forms of music pedagogy and ensemble interaction, while retaining some traditional features, have undergone significant changes, which are related to broader issues of change in contemporary Turkish society. Fourth: the performance and construction of Anatolian musical instruments today are linked with national, local, and regional identities, and with the ensemble and recorded arrangements of traditional and art musics.

Concepts of place and space, in particular the interplay between national, regional, and local identities, have had profound effects on musical practices in Anatolia and have been profoundly affected by musical practice as well. While certain dances, musical instruments, and song forms are found only within a small area and are local in nature, others became nationalized via state ensembles, radio and TV broadcasts, and a government campaign to create a national consciousness about Turkey's different regions. This resulted in a government archive of over fifty thousand *türkü*-s (Turkish language, unauthored folk songs), a key topic of Chapter 1. Similar governmental sponsorship came later to urban music, and the *şarkı* song form became symbolic of cosmopolitan Istanbul (Chapters 2 and 4). Localities, regions, and transnational ideas also are central themes in political music in Turkey, surfacing in folk poetry written in honor of the founder of the Turkish Republic, songs protesting against governmental corruption, songs that espouse socialist politics through the life histories of Ottoman-era folk heroes, and finally the story of one of the best known and most contested folk songs, "Sarı Gelin / Sari Gyalin" (Chapter 5). Numerous technologies have been instrumental in the transmission of rural and urban musical styles. However, each has affected the performance practice of music to varying degrees. With the introduction of Western-style staff notation to rural music, songs that formerly had a flexible sense of timing became static and visualized in relation to European conceptions of musical time. The *usul* system (Chapter 3), a long-standing indigenous conceptualization of musical time, continues to be used, but the aesthetics and practice of *usul* have also changed. Audio recording began in Turkey around 1899, and many of Tanburi Cemil Bey's early solo instrumental recordings have since become the most imitated exemplars of the performance practice of urban art music (Chapter 2). Since the late 1990s, multitrack digital audio-recording technologies have become central tools in the production and modernization of arranged folk and Anatolian ethnic music (Chapter 4).

The social nature of music making—how the concept of conversation structures Anatolian music, how music is taught and transmitted, and how musical ensembles interact—is a primary theme in the experience of music in contemporary Turkey. One of the main aspects of musical form in most Anatolian music styles is an ongoing dialogue between two musical parts, known as the *soru* (question) and *cevap* (answer), a key topic in Chapters 3 and 4. In the musical life of the Alevis (a heterodox religious order found throughout Anatolia), music was both taught and performed in the semiformal "conversational" gathering known as *muhabbet* (Chapter 1). *Meşk*, a similar traditional pedagogical context for urban art music, underwent subtle changes when it became the primary choral-singing teaching method in neighborhood musical associations (Chapter 2). Before the 1930s, music was not performed in large ensembles in Turkey, but within a couple decades there were folk- and art-music orchestras and large choruses. Chapter 4 examines the process of arrangement, whereby formerly solo or small-ensemble styles are adapted into staged ensemble performances or simulated ensembles concocted in the recording studio.

Musical instruments are not just objects of historical interest or tools for music making: they are windows into society, history, and technology. Turkey is arguably the Middle Eastern and Central Asian center for instrument production, exporting instruments to Azerbaijan, the Arabian Peninsula, Iran, Europe, and North America. Through a comparison of two *saz*-makers and one oud-maker, I explore questions of instrument construction, forest management, and the effect of increasing international trade on local craft industries, and examine how contemporary musicians and changing musical aesthetics have driven changes to musical-instrument design (Chapters 1 and 2). I look at why the long-necked *bağlama-saz* came to have such a strong role in twentieth-century Turkish nationalism, while its shorter-necked cousin, the Alevi *dedesaz*, had no nationalist associations but considerable significance as a sacred instrument. I compare two urban art-music instruments—the *tanbur,* believed to be a quintessentially Turkish urban art-music instrument, and the oud, perceived as Greek, Arab, or Kurdish, even when performed by ethnically Turkish oudists (Chapter 2). I explore how two fiddles of Greek origin—the *lyra politiki* and the *Pontos lyra*—became Turkish classical and Turkish/Laz folk instruments, both called *kemençe.* New instruments continue to be invented in Turkey, too. The *perdesiz gitar,* a special fretless acoustic guitar invented by Erkan Oğur, is now effectively an Anatolian instrument and used for playing a variety of traditional and art-music styles (Chapter 4).

Aficionados of Turkish music will immediately note a number of musical styles and instruments that are not covered in the present volume. My goal is not to provide an exhaustive overview of music genres in Turkey but rather to render audible the connections between traditional practices and contemporary arranged popular music by covering key instruments and traditions in as much depth as this little volume permits. I do not cover wind instruments such as the *ney, kaval, zurna, tulum,* and *mey*; the *kanun* zither; and many percussion varieties. I focus on plucked and bowed lutes, as they represent the most ubiquitous instrument family in Turkey, are used in the widest variety of musical styles, and present a primary challenge for the student attempting to differentiate the sounds and social meanings of the myriad lute-family instruments. The *Music in Egypt* volume of this series has an excellent introduction to the *nay* (*ney*), *mizmar* (similar to *zurna*; see also Bryant 1991), and *qanun* (*kanun*). While not identical to their Anatolian counterparts, they are similar in sound and construction. The *Music in Bulgaria* volume discusses the *kaval* flute and the *gaida* (which are related to the Anatolian *kaval* and the Eastern Black Sea *tulum* bagpipes; see also Ahrens 1973).

ABOUT THE LISTENING CD

The majority of the listening-CD selections are excerpts of recordings released by Istanbul-based Kalan Müzik and readily available internationally. Kalan is an extraordinary label that has released many of the most significant contemporary arranged folk- and art-music recordings, has sponsored extensive fieldwork projects on Anatolian ethnic musics, and is responsible for keeping high-quality reissues of historically important archival recordings of art and folk music in print. Due to excessive licensing costs, I was unable to include several key recordings from other record labels on the enclosed listening CD.

PRONUNCIATION, SPELLING, AND GRAMMAR

The Turkish alphabet has twenty-nine letters—twenty-one consonants and eight vowels. Six have no corresponding character in the Latin alphabet—the consonants ç, ş, and ğ, and the vowels ö, ü, and ı. Others, such as c, o, and u, do have a corresponding character, but differ phonetically to English usage. Vowels with circumflexes (e.g., âşik) are sometimes used in words of Arabic and Persian origin and typically indicate a slight lengthening of the vowel.

c	As the " j" in jump
ç/Ç	As the "ch" in cheese
ş/Ş	As the "sh" in she
ğ/Ğ	Lengthens the preceding vowel
a	As the "a" in far
e	As the "e" in send
i/İ	As the "ee" in seed
ı/I	As the "a" in about
o	As the "o" in so
ö/Ö	As the "er" in her
u	As the "oo" in boot
ü/Ü	As the "eu" in lieu. Close to the German ü.

Examples: *bağlama* (a long-necked lute) is pronounced "baaah-lah-ma." *Cevap* ("answer") is pronounced "jeh-vahp." *Meşk* (a traditional pedagogical style) is pronounced "meh-shk." *Şarkı* ("song") is pronounced "shark-uh."

When possible, spelling conventions for musical terminology are based on Yılmaz Öztuna's *Türk Musikisi Ansiklopedik Sözlüğü* (2006 edition). Although there is disagreement in Turkey about the use of circumflex characters to indicate words of Persian and Arabic origin (e.g., *tanbûrî, semâî*), I use them only when their absence implies a different word altogether (e.g. *âşık*, "wandering minstrel," which is unrelated to *aşık*, "anklebone"), and for Kurdish- and Zazaki-language long vowels. I employ the postfix "-s" to make plurals from Turkish nouns (*kemençe*-s). In Turkish, plurals are normally created by adding the *-lar* or *-ler* suffix but are used less frequently than their English-language counterparts. Additionally, when making compound nouns, Turkish requires the use of a postfix on the second noun. For example, combining the word *saz* (instrument) with *semai* (a beat structure) yields *saz semaisi*, while *Türk* (Turk) with *aksak* (limping) with *usul* (beat structure) yields <u>*Türk aksağı*</u> <u>*usulu*</u>. Finally, the *ci/cı/cu/cü* suffix is commonly added to nouns to indicate someone who is a maker of, or a professional who uses, that object (*davulcu* = professional *davul* player). For a comprehensive treatment of modern Turkish grammar, see Aslı Göksel and Celia Kerslake's *Turkish: A Comprehensive Grammar* (2005).

ACKNOWLEDGMENTS

This volume would not have been possible without the support of series editors Bonnie Wade, who provided encouragement and repeat careful readings from the initial proposal through the submission of the final draft and her collective wisdom from overseeing this monumental series, and Pat Campbell, who shared excellent suggestions on the pedagogical framing of the work. Three anonymous reviewers provided exceptionally productive, considerate, and spot-on comments. I'd like to thank Virginia Danielson, Harvard University; Theodore Levin, Dartmouth College; Scott Marcus, University of California—Santa Barbara; Irene Markoff, York University; Anne K. Rasmussen, The College of William and Mary; and Martin Stokes, St. John's College, Oxford. Ladi Dell'aira supported this effort in uncountable ways, particularly in undertaking the bulk of photography, assisting with interviews, managing travel in Turkey, editing the manuscript, and providing unending moral support. At Oxford University Press, Cory Schneider, Jan Beatty, and Jennifer Bossert saw the manuscript through to final production. I also thank Benjamin Brinner for advising and supporting my research from the predissertation stage through to this book.

Nine scholar/musicians in Turkey played an especially important role in my research into recording studios, arrangement, and rural musics. Mustafa Avcı shared his expertise on *saz*-family instruments xviii ∞ PREFACE

and pedagogy and graciously helped review song translations. Ayşenur Kolivar generously shared her personal archive of field recordings and expertise on Karadeniz music and dance cultures, and provided hospitality during our travels to the Black Sea. At Kalan Records, Hasan Saltık kindly provided permissions for the use of the Kalan music and photo archives. Ulaş Özdemir facilitated studio access (and provided the privilege of recording his album, *Bu Dem*) and also gave considerable insight into contemporary Alevi culture and musical practice. While engineering for Aytekin Ataş, Fatih Yaşar, and Yılmaz Yeşilyurt, I learned much about the cultures of arrangement and the development of the recorded genre of Anatolian ethnic music. Yeliz Keskin graciously allowed the use of her photographs, provided us hospitality in Istanbul and Sümela, and engaged in discussions about Karadeniz and Laz culture. Ömer Avcı introduced the world of Anatolian percussion in arranged Alevi and Kurdish music. These individuals all provided unwavering long-term support for this research.

Two teacher-mentors inspired me to start nearly two decades of research. In 1992, Scott Marcus handed me an oud and a stack of sheet music, thereby opening the world of Arab music and culture. He provided detailed feedback on this volume, and the presentation of musical-theoretical concepts was greatly enhanced from this feedback. My oud and *makam hocası* Necati Çelik invited me to study in Turkey, encouraged me to observe the rehearsals of the Istanbul State Turkish Music Ensemble, and graciously provided private lessons since 1993.

I wish to thank numerous individuals in Istanbul who assisted with this project. At ZB Stüdyo: Soner Akalın, Neriman Güneş, Metin Kalaç, Eyüp Hamiş, Ertan Tekin, Serkan Çağrı, and Metin Yılmaz were wonderful to work with and to discuss Istanbul's studio work cultures with. Ladi and I thank Sabahat Akkiraz, Aynur Doğan, and Aysun Doğan for stimulating interviews that gave a personal perspective on, respectively, Alevi *muhabbet* culture and Kurdish women's music traditions. At the Üsküdar Musiki Cemiyeti, Aslı Akoba facilitated visits and participation in *meşk* and engaged in a heartfelt discussion of the meaning of *sanat* music and the role of the *cemiyet*, and Cahit Deniz passionately discussed *cemiyet* pedagogy and *meşk* with me. At Istanbul Technical University, Şehvar Besiroğlu invited me into her *makam* theory course, and Robert Reigle provided institutional support and stimulating conversations about *dengbêj* vocal styles. Special thanks to Inan Altın and the members of Grup Yorum for sharing the experience of recording *Yıldızlar Kuşandık*; İlknur Yakupoğlu for her hospitality in Ankara and for an inspiring evening of *kemençe* music and conversation; Ender

Abadoğlu for discussions of folklore, politics, and the musical influences on contemporary arranged music; Nail Yurtsever for opening Stüdyo Sound to my research; and Engin Arslan for illuminating the *saz* pedagogy of *dershane*-s. I thank Ergül Sönmez for discussions of local music styles from Tunceli and for the many memorable nights at Victoria Lokantası; Sinan Erdemsel for insight into *makam* theory and Mevlevi and Sinani Sufi music; Bob Beer for logistical help and conversations about *saz* pedagogy; and Arzu Öztürkmen for her inspiring words on the history of Turkish folklore. Luthiers Özbek Uçar, Hasan Sarıkaya, and Ramazan Calay kindly shared insights into the world of instrument making and opened up their shops to Ladi and me.

Outside of Turkey, we thank Richard Anderson for his mentoring in digital-image workflow. Larry Witzleben, Jocelyne Guilbault, and Graham St John all provided moral support and friendship at various stages in the project. We also thank the Bates and Dell'aira clans for their encouragement and assistance with innumerable things. My research was facilitated in part by a State Department Fellowship generously provided by ARIT (American Research Institute in Turkey) (2006–2007), a Fulbright IIE grant (2005–2006), and financial support from UC Berkeley and Wesleyan University.

Introduction

∽

Music in contemporary Turkey is inextricably linked to the history of the Republic of Turkey and the complex histories of the Ottoman Empire and numerous other empires that preceded it. By the tenth century, when the first Oghuz Turks descended from Transoxania (in present-day Kazakhstan and Uzbekistan) towards the Byzantine-governed Anatolian plains, the land that was to become their home had already experienced the Greek wars, as told in Homer's *Iliad*, much of which took place in Anatolia. Anatolia had also been home to the Akkadian Empire (twenty-fourth century BCE), various Hittite empires (from the fourteenth century BCE), the Roman conquests of Constantine the Great (the early fourth century AD), and numerous dynasties including the Kingdom of Armenia (190 BCE–387 AD), the Empire of Nicaea (1204–1261), and the Empire of Trebizond (1204–1461).

The Ottoman Empire (1302–1922), at its peak in the seventeenth century, controlled most of Southeast Europe, West Asia, and North Africa, administering a land of incredible cultural and linguistic diversity. Rather than assimilating the many cultures they governed, the Ottomans governed through the *millet* system, whereby members of religiously defined ethnicities lived in separate city neighborhoods, managed their own judicial systems, and collected their own taxes. The primary *millet*-s were Muslim, Greek Orthodox, Jewish, Armenian (divided into Apostolic, Catholic, and Protestant Armenians), and Syriac Orthodox. In rural areas, villages were demarcated by both religion and language.

In response to the decline of the Ottoman Empire and the growth of nationalism in Europe and in Russia, a Turkish nationalist movement began in the late nineteenth century, culminating in the establishment of the Republic of Turkey (1923). One tenet of Turkish nationalism was the historical link between the different Turkic tribes, and a perceived brotherhood between Turks, Azeris, Uzbeks, and Turkmens. Another was the creation of a modern Turkish language (purged of Arabic and Persian loanwords) as the sole national language of the Turkish Republic.

Turkishness was a cultural identity available to anyone born in Turkey who had a Turkish name and was nominally Muslim, regardless of his or her past family ethnic identity. Folklore research and the national dissemination of folklore (particularly, rural folk music) were integral to the formation of the modern Turkish identity.

By the end of the twentieth century, assimilationist policies had resulted in Turkish being the first language of nearly all Turkish citizens. However, numerous ethnicities continued to live in Turkey. Based on the research of Peter Andrews (1989), forty-six (perhaps even more) different ethnicities exist within the present republic, many of which continue to live in isolated and distinct villages. While Kurds, Armenians, and Rom gypsies have received worldwide attention, ethnicities such as the Laz or Hemşin are scarcely known even inside Turkey. Ethnicity in Turkey is a very complex topic, as many Turkish citizens self-identify as being members of more than one ethnicity. For example, Zazaki-speaking Alevis may situationally choose to self-identify as Turks, as Zazas (a linguistic distinction), as Alevi (a religious distinction), or possibly even as Kurds. While in the early 1990s it had been nearly impossible to find recordings or performances of music in languages other than Turkish, by the year 2000 numerous record labels specialized in the music of Anatolian ethnicities.

Throughout this book, I use the term **Anatolia** to refer to the West Asian subcontinent located within the borders of the Republic of Turkey, and **Anatolian** to describe instruments or musical practices that are ethnically ambiguous or shared amongst several ethnicities in Anatolia. **Turkish music** specifically means songs sung in the Turkish language, regardless of musical style. **Turkic** refers to cultural elements perceived as shared among speakers of Turkish, Azeri, Kazakh, Uyghur, and around thirty linguistically related Asian languages.

The primary generic distinction I make in this book is between **rural** and **urban** musics and instruments, with a secondary distinction between folk and art musics. Local folk songs, dance musics, religious or sacred musics, and more esoteric art-music traditions exist both in rural Anatolia and in the cities of Istanbul, Ankara, and Izmir (Figure I.1). Some of the oldest surviving musical repertoire is not urban art music but rather the Persian-inspired poetry of sixteenth-century *âşık* poets, such as Pir Sultan Abdal, that continues to be performed today by Alevi musicians in rural Central and Eastern Anatolia (CD track 1). Art musicians in Istanbul often include *İstanbul türküsü*—folk ballads from Istanbul—in their concerts of urban art music.

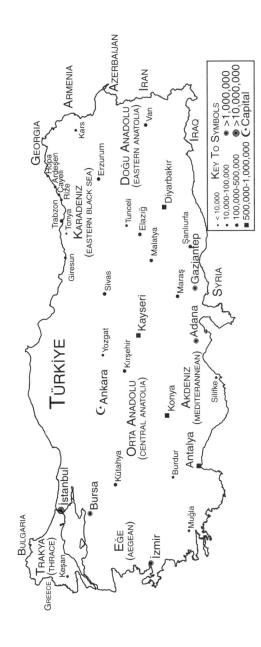

FIGURE I.1 Republic of Turkey, showing town, city, and region names referred to in the text.

The rural-urban distinction is also important for drawing attention to the sudden encounter between rural Anatolia and Turkey's cities in the aftermath of the foundation of the Turkish Republic. Shortly after the birth of the republic, government-funded institutes facilitated administrative and cultural links between Anatolian villages and the nation's two modern cities—Istanbul and Ankara. Mehmet Ziya Gökalp (1876–1924), the "father" of Turkish nationalism, along with Mustafa Kemal Atatürk (1881–1938), the founder of the Turkish Republic, believed that modern Turks should simultaneously be European citizens and embrace the customs and morals of the peasants of rural Anatolia. The formation of national radio and TV, conservatories, and urban-based folk-music orchestras encouraged new kinds of interactions between rural musicians and musics and their urban counterparts.

Following the establishment of a multiparty political system in 1950, the most significant manifestation of the rural-urban dichotomy has been the massive influx of immigrants from rural areas into cities. In Istanbul, the population grew from 980,000 (1950) to 12.6 million (2008), with an unofficial population estimated at 20 million. Some Istanbul suburbs attracted significant numbers of immigrants from particular regions of Turkey (for example, many Alevis from the Central Anatolian province of Sivas emigrated to Istanbul's Okmeydanı neighborhood) (Figure I.2). Rather than wholly abandoning traditional ways, rural immigrants often continue their musical practices within a new,

FIGURE I.2 *Map of Istanbul showing all discussed neighborhoods and primary landmarks.*

densely urban context, and new circuits of cultural production connect Anatolian rural localities with Istanbul. However, due to extreme urban density, Istanbul's residents experience an immense variety of musical forms, including other local rural musics, urban art and folk music, popular music, and foreign musics.

CD Track List

Unless otherwise noted, CD examples are used courtesy of the Kalan Müzik Archive with the permission of Hasan Saltık.

1. Muharrem Ertaş, "Kalktı Göç Eyledi." From *Kalktı Göç Eyledi* (Kalan CD 112, © 1998).
2. Tolga Çandar, "Karyolamın Demiri." From *Türküleri Ege'nin III* (Kalan CD 227, © 2001).
3. Âşık Veysel, "Atatürk'e Ağıt." From *Âşık Veysel* (Kalan CD 235, © 2001).
4. Fatih Yaşar, "Sabahtan Kalkan Kızlar." From *Kıyıların Ardı* (Kalan CD 439, © 2008).
5. Dertli Divani, "Zamanı Gelir." From *Hasbihâl* (Kalan CD 337, © 2005).
6. Cem Karaca, "Dadaloğlu." From *Cemaz-ul Evvel* (Kalan CD 18, © 1994).
7. Ulaş Özdemir, "Âşık Oldur." From *Bu Dem* (Kalan CD 453, © 2008).
8. Erkan Oğur & İsmail Hakkı Demircioğlu, "Ey Zahit Şaraba." From *Anadolu Beşik* (Kalan CD 178, © 2000).
9. İlknur Yakupoğlu & Ayşenur Kolivar, "Oy Trabzon." (Live recording, May 2007). Used by permission of the artists.
10. Grup Helesa, "Sümela." (Live recording, August 2005). Used by permission of Ayşenur Kolivar.
11. Kâni Karaca, "Saba Âyîni 1. Selam." From *Mevlana: Dede Efendi Saba Âyîni* (Kalan CD 42, © 1996).
12. Kültür Bakanlığı İstanbul Devlet Klasik Türk Müziği Korosu & Nevzat Atlığ, "Mahrum-i Şevkim." From *Türk Musikisinden Seçmeler: Itri'den Suphi Ziya Ökbekkan'a* (Kalan CD 358, © 2006).
13. Istanbul State Turkish Music Ensemble, "Bir Gizli Günahın." (Live recording, March 1996).

xxvii

14. Yorgo Bacanos, "Hüseyni Taksim." From *Yorgo Bacanos 1900–1977* (Kalan CD 66, © 1997).

15. Necati Çelik, "Muhayyerkürdi Saz Semaisi" by Reşat Aysu. (Live recording, April 2003). Used by permission of Necati Çelik.

16. Zeki Müren "Bir Bahar Akşamı." From *Selahattin Pınar Şarkıları* (Kalan CD 353, © 2005).

17. Necdet Yaşar, "Bestenigar Saz Semaisi." From *Necdet Yaşar 2* (Kalan CD 273, © 2003).

18. Selim Sesler, "Kiremit Bacaları." From *Keşan'a Giden Yollarlarda* (Kalan CD 154, © 1999).

19. Sadettin Kaynak "Akşam Oldu Yine Bastı Kareler." From *Kendi Sesinden Hafız Sadettin Kaynak* (Kalan CD 129, © 1999).

20. Tanburi Cemil Bey, "Eviç Taksim." From *Tanburi Cemil Bey* (Kalan CD 25, © 1995).

21. İncesaz (with Dilek Türkan), "Tereddüt." From *Dört/Mazi Kalbimde* (Kalan CD 359, © 2005).

22. Fatih Yaşar, "Lazepeşi Duğuni." From *Kıyıların Ardı* (Kalan CD 439, © 2008).

23. Şevval Sam, "Bu Dünya Bir Pencere." From *Karadeniz* (Kalan CD 454, © 2008).

24. Marsis, "Bu Dünya Bir Pencere." From *Marsis* (Kalan CD 470, © 2009).

25. Aynur, "Keçe Kurdan." From *Keçe Kurdan* (Kalan CD 293, © 2004).

26. Mikaîl Aslan, "Îqrardar." From *Zernkut* (Kalan CD 434, © 2008).

27. Dengbêj Fadil, "Seydik." From *Eyhok: Hakkari Geleneksel Müziği* (Kalan CD 318, © 2004).

28. Erkan Oğur, "Çayın Öte Yüzünde." From *Bir Ömürlük Misafır* (Kalan CD 184, © 2000).

29. Telvin, "İki Anahtar." From *Telvin* (Kalan CD 364, © 2006).

30. Grup Yorum, "Kavuşma." From *Yıldızlar Kuşandık* (Kalan CD 374, © 2006).

31. Kardeş Türküler, "Sari Gyalin" [Armenian]. From *Kardeş Türküler* (Kalan CD 62, © 1997).

32. Hossein Alizadeh, "Sari Galin" [Azeri]. From *Endless Vision* (World Village 468047, © 2005).

CHAPTER 1

Anatolian Rural Musics and Instruments

It's midnight on a Thursday night at Umut Türkü Evi, a *türkü* bar in the Beyoğlu neighborhood of Istanbul. On a small and cramped raised stage, a band performs a wide range of music, mostly audience requests, but particularly *türkü*—Turkish-language folk songs from rural Anatolia (Section 1). Maroon vinyl-covered booths line both walls, small round tables and chairs consume much of the floor, and inside the long and narrow bar are some forty customers, a mix of men and women ranging from single twenty-somethings to retired businessmen. At one table, six people with familial origins in villages near Izmir (a city on the Aegean coast) enthusiastically sing along and sway in time with the music as the band performs "Karyolamın Demiri" (CD track 2). Their voices nearly drown out the band's lead singer—a feat, considering that she sings into a heavily amplified sound system. Another table (a group of customers that came together) has just scribbled three requests on a napkin—two *türkü*-s from Diyarbakır (a city in Southeastern Anatolia) and one *halay* dance song—which they pass to the band's *saz*-player (Section 4). Within a minute, the band's keyboardist has picked up an *askı-davul* drum (Section 7) and launches into the *halay*, and the table who requested the *halay* jump to their feet and start a line dance in the middle of the bar. One young man in a pinstriped suit leads the line, enthusiastically waving a handkerchief in his right hand. As the evening progresses, the band covers repertoire from nearly every region of Turkey, including slow sentimental songs, fast dance pieces, and everything in between. Umut Türkü Evi hired these musicians because they have a shared repertoire of over 1500 songs they can perform from memory. On some evenings, however, they get to perform suites that feature the music they know best—Alevi sacred/secular repertoire from Sivas in Central Anatolia (Section 3).

The Umut Türkü Evi is one of perhaps over a thousand *türkü* bars in the city of Istanbul alone (many such establishments exist elsewhere in Turkey, too). Why is the singing of rural folk music, even musics with origins in remote agrarian localities, so popular in the world's fifth-largest city? How did *türkü* singing become a widespread practice, and why is the *saz* such an important instrument in rural song performance today, even in performing musics that once were not accompanied by the *saz*? What does *türkü* singing and *halay* dancing mean to the customers of Umut Türkü Evi? To begin to answer these questions, I will turn to the 1920s, when the Republic of Turkey was born and musical practices from rural Anatolia became integral to the establishment of a concept of Turkish identity.

1.1 RURAL SONG FORMS: *TÜRKÜ* AND *UZUN HAVA*

In the 1920s, Mustafa Kemal Atatürk, the father of the modern Republic of Turkey, mandated the collecting of Turkish-language folk songs from across Anatolia through government-sponsored folklore projects. So important were these projects that Béla Bartók (1881–1945), the famed Hungarian composer and folklorist, was employed in 1935–1936 to conduct a major expedition (Bartók 2002 [1976]) in the Adana Province of southeastern Turkey and to teach younger Turkish folklorists how to collect, transcribe, and analyze folk songs. He left a collection of precisely detailed notations and song analyses that continues to be important to this day. Ahmed Adnan Saygun (1907–1991), who like Bartók was a composer of new music, trained with Bartók in folk-song collection and transcription and went on to influence how folk-song notation was done in Turkey. After Bartók left, similar expeditions continued under Saygun and other folklorists. A newly formed entity, the Village Institutes, expanded the scope and reach of folklore activities by sponsoring music competitions around the country and encouraging local artists to participate. These competitions, and amateur folk-song collections organized by the Village Institutes, resulted in the transcription and archiving of tens of thousands of song notations.

The primary genre of collected songs became the center of a government-managed music repertoire known as *türkü*, which loosely translates to "Turkish-language ballad." To become a *türkü*, a song needed to be sung in Turkish and not suspected of having religious functions or meanings. Numerous songs performed in Kurdish, Armenian, Lazuri, Zazaki, and other indigenous languages were either not recorded or were translated or adapted on the spot into a Turkish version. Although some *türkü* are probably similar today in melody and lyrics to the initially collected version, in many instances lyrics were changed, melodies simplified, and rhythmic variations standardized. Unfortunately, the notes left by folklorists do not always reveal if, or how, they adapted particular songs. It is also important to note that even for *türkü*-s sung in Turkish today, many continue to be well known in other languages (see Chapter 5 for a discussion of one such song, "Sarı Gelin").

One persistent myth about folk music, particularly *türkü*-s and the dance works discussed later in this chapter, is that works are authorless. Since Anatolian peasants did not *notate* music, and since most folklorists working in Turkey did not routinely inquire of the peasants if the songs they collected were composed by the singer or the singer's family, it was assumed that peasants did not write or compose music. In keeping with theories of folklore and the creative life of peasants that had been established in Germany, Russia, and the Balkans several decades earlier, the imagined lives of peasants included folk arts that were assumed to be quintessentially timeless, not newly created. These theories greatly influenced the development of indigenous folklore in Turkey, to the extent that ongoing compositional practices found through much of rural Anatolia became much less valued than the performance of supposedly authorless works.

The question arises then: where did all of these folk songs come from? In *âşık* poetic forms and Alevi sacred and secular music (Sections 2 and 3), poets refer to themselves and assert authorship in the final verse. If the last verse is lost in retelling (or was not transcribed by the folklorist for some reason), the song is rendered authorless. Another practice that continues to this day is that of singers adding verses to preexisting songs. During my research in Istanbul recording studios, most professional singers I met had written their own verses to well-known *türkü*, and those verses sometimes became as well known as older verses or even replaced them in common practice. However, Turkish copyright law (and other performing artists) only officially recognize authorship if the first verse of a work is unambiguously authored. Singers continue to expand the scope and meaning of *türkü* by adding verses, but this practice is not remembered as authorship or individual creativity.

The performer or passionate fan of Turkish-language folk music may know one thousand or more *türkü*-s from all over Anatolia. Interestingly, connoisseurs know not only the melody, rhythm, and lyrics but the locality or region of origin, the name of the folklorist who collected the song, and the name of the performer who sang for the original source recording. This memory is aided by (though not solely attributable to) published *türkü* songbooks, which are usually organized in alphabetical order by the first stanza of lyrics but have indexes sorted by region and sometimes by folklorist. Other song collections focus on the songs of only one region and are indexed by locality.

In Istanbul today, *türkü*-s are most often performed at *türkü* bars, small nightclubs that serve *rakı* (anise liqueur), beer, and nonalcoholic beverages (Figure 1.1). Istanbul's hundreds of *türkü* bars are concentrated in the Beyoğlu, Kadıköy, Aksaray, and Bakırköy neighborhoods (Figure P.2). Similar venues exist across Turkey. Performances range from one person playing *saz* and singing, to five-person groups performing some combination of *saz* (see Section 4), guitar, violin, clarinet, end-blown flutes, percussion, and drum machines and synthesizers that mimic the aforementioned acoustic instruments. Often, each table is occupied by patrons from a specific locality, and they may request that the group perform specific songs from a town or village, or generically a suite of music from that locality. *Türkü*-bar musicians need to know a vast variety of repertoire from all over Turkey and are expected to play pieces in a regionally appropriate manner. The *dershane* training that *bağlama* players receive (see Section 4) thus feeds perfectly into this performance demand.

Some *türkü*-s have lyric variants, and I witnessed numerous disputes in *türkü* bars about which version of the *türkü* was the most authentic or correct. *Türkü* fans may be able to list all the nationally known star performers who have sung any well-known variant of the song. In my own experiences singing *türkü* in Istanbul for local audiences, I would often be approached during set breaks by patrons who would take a pen to my lyrics sheets, crossing off "errant" phrases and replacing them with the "correct" lyrics (even when I had obtained lyrics from the official government notation archives). Other times, people attending *türkü* bars would bring their own songbooks, prepared to sing along with anything the group might perform.

FIGURE 1.1   Türkü *bar district of Beyoğlu, Istanbul.*   *(Photo by Ladi Dell'aira)*

The term *türkü* today encompasses numerous genres of songs, including unmetered laments and ballads (*uzun hava*, lit. "long air"), metered songs (*kırık hava*, lit. "broken air"), and dance songs (*oyun havası*, lit. "dance air") (Chapter 3 covers the concept of musical time and meter in Anatolian music). All four terms—*türkü, uzun hava, kırık hava, oyun havası*—are newcomers to Anatolian folk-music vocabulary and are primarily used in Istanbul and Ankara by urban musicians and scholars to describe rural folk musics. In the respective localities from where these repertoires hail, a term like *türkü* is meaningless, and more specific terms are used. For example, the *bozlak* is a special kind of *uzun hava* found in the Kırşehir, Yozgat and Ankara provinces of Central Anatolia and the Adana Province of the Mediterranean Region and is sung by Abdal and Avşar *âşık* poets such as Muharrem Ertaş (1913–1984, CD track 1). *Bozlak* differs in poetic form, lyrical meaning, dramatic tension, and performance style from other local *uzun*

hava varieties such as the Black Sea *destan* or the Alevi *divan*, or from the *açış*, an instrumental introduction to a vocal song that draws on vocal *uzun hava* styles. Likewise, the term *kırık hava* conflates unrelated genres such as lullabies, laments (*ağıt*, CD track 3), exile songs, and love songs (*aşk/sevda türküsü*, CD track 4) and is also unspecific with regard to poetic meter or rhyming schema.

You may be wondering how to make sense of this bewildering array of different song genres, region names, and cultural descriptors. The main point to take away from the preceding passage is that one of the defining features of music in rural Anatolia is the staggering variety of local and regional genres. Although *türkü* became nationalized in the twentieth century, the hundreds of genres that comprise a national repertoire continue to be highly localized and stylistically different. However, not all rural songs are today classified as *türkü*. I turn now to *âşık* poetry and Alevi music, traditions that feature authored poetry.

1.2   *ÂŞIK* POETRY AND POETS

Âşık—"one who is in love"—refers to practitioners of a wide range of musical and poetic practices, most involving one or two musicians singing while playing *saz* (Section 4), and *uzun hava* or *kırık hava* song forms. In some *âşık* traditions, the poet-singer is a wandering minstrel who travels across Anatolia and Central Asia. In others, such as traditions in Kars and Erzurum in Eastern Anatolia, two or more *âşık*-s improvise poetry in song duels. Some traditions are known for particularly potent political commentary, while others involve praise singing, or poetry dealing with more heroic or metaphysical themes. Most *âşık* poets come from the Abdal, Avşar, or Turkmen tribes—three Turkic tribes that live in villages throughout West and Central Asia.

Even though not all *âşık*-s are professional wandering minstrels, travel is a very important part of the life of an *âşık*, including travel to study with *âşık*-s in other Turkic-speaking communities and travel to *âşık* festivals that happen throughout Anatolia. For example, in the mid-1800s, the song-dueling *âşık* tradition of Kars and Erzurum had completely died out, and Âşık Şenlik (1853–1912) traveled to Baku, Tbilisi, and Yerevan (today the capitals respectively of Azerbaijan, Georgia, and Armenia) to study with Azeri-speaking *âşık*-s (Erdener 1995, 32). On his return, he reestablished the song-dueling tradition, which continues to this day. Other *âşık*-s traveled as far as Kazakhstan in order to learn specific performing styles. *Âşık* traditions are quintessentially Turkic and transcend state boundaries, and have for hundreds of years involved a flow of peoples throughout the Turkish-, Turkmen-, and Azeri-speaking world.

Folklorist Yıldıray Erdener wrote the most extensive English-language ethnography of the Kars *âşık* culture, an exclusively male tradition performed mainly in coffeehouses but occasionally at national *âşık* festivals. The multiethnic clientele, including Turkmen, Kurdish, Azeri, and Turkish Sunni and Shi'ite guests, all had their own preferred melodies and song themes, and a skilled *âşık* could read the audience for each performance before choosing themes, musical ideas, and even poetic forms (Erdener 1995, 82–83). One especially challenging song-duel type involved both *âşık*-s propping their mouths open with pins or toothpicks. This prevented them from articulating labial consonants and made their process of improvising poetry much more difficult.

Unlike *türkü*, which is thought of today as authorless and timeless "folk music," *âşık* poetry is authored and composed, and an *âşık* usually inserts his or her own name in the last verse of a poem. Some *âşık*-s, through their songs, even keep an oral narrative of the lives and works of previous generations of *âşık*-s, and thus today we know of *âşık* poetry from over five hundred years ago. Some *âşık*-s kept notebooks filled with poems, but for the most part, poems and songs were orally transmitted, kept alive with apprenticeships and later through institutions like the Kars coffeehouse song competitions. In most *âşık* traditions, songs mix historical and contemporary themes. A common poetic subject matter is the deeds of folk heroes, which in its retelling often takes on a strongly political message. For example, many contemporary *âşık*-s sing of the life history and political ideology of Pir Sultan Abdal (sixteenth century), rural Anatolia's "Robin Hood," who fought against Ottoman authoritarianism and was ultimately hung for his resistance. They also sing of the deeds of Hacı Bektaş Veli (thirteenth century), who during his life was the patron saint and uniting force of the Turkmen communities in Eastern Anatolia and present-day Iran, and who continues to be the most important saint for Alevis (see the next section).

This tradition of singing the praises of legendary leaders extends to more recent ones as well. In Chapter 5 I will discuss a lament composed by Âşık Veysel in 1938 on the occasion of the death of Mustafa Kemal Atatürk (CD track 3). In the twenty-first century, new generations of *âşık*-s sing about socialism, European Union accession, American imperialism, and other relevant contemporary political themes.

1.3 ALEVI SACRED/SECULAR MUSIC

Of the seventy-one million Turkish citizens today who are officially registered in the census as having Muslim faith, 15 to 20 percent are Alevis. Alevism is both an ethnicity and a heterodox religious order, which has ancient roots in the shamanic practices of Anatolia and Central Asia and has influences from the ancient religion of Zoroastrianism. During the time of Shah Ismail and the foundation of the Iranian Safavid Dynasty in the early 1600s, Alevism adopted many practices and beliefs from Shi'a Islam, the denomination of Islam most widely practiced today in Iran, Iraq, and Azerbaijan.

Although Alevis recognize the Qur'an as a sacred text, Mohammed as a prophet, and Mohammed's son-in-law, Ali, as the successor to Mohammed, they do not follow many of the practices of other Muslims, eschewing mosque rituals, fasting during Ramadan, the *namaz* prayer done five times a day, and the prohibitions on alcohol and music. (For discussion of prohibitions on music in some Islamic contexts, see Marcus 2007, the volume on Egypt in this Global Music Series.) Instead, *cem* (Alevi worship) is a social gathering and ritual involving music and dance that takes place at a *cemevi* (worship house). Alevism places a stronger emphasis on accountability and the actions of individuals than on their beliefs, and Alevi poetry evokes a sentiment that is similar to Western humanist thought. When the Turkish Republic was founded in 1923, Alevis were some of the most ardent supporters of its secular principles, and of its architect Mustafa Kemal Atatürk, whose portrait is often hung in *cemevi*-s next to those of Hacı Bektaş Veli (the thirteenth-century saint mentioned above) and other important saints.

ACTIVITY 1.1 *Hacı Bektaş Veli had a great importance in the history of the Ottoman Empire. Using Internet resources, research Hacı Bektaş's life and the time in which he lived. What powers controlled the region? What was his role in the foundation of the Ottoman Empire? How did he become a saint? What does his life story mean to modern-day Alevis?*

I wrote earlier about Alevism as an ethnicity. The broader topic of ethnicity in modern Turkey, and the specificity of Alevi ethnicity, is a complex topic. First, it is imperative to understand that the term *ethnicity* became widely used in the English language in the 1970s in order to theorize cultural groups that self-identify on the basis of one or more shared traits (including but not limited to language, religion, territory, historical tribal affiliation, or endogamic tendencies). However, two important historical factors continue to strongly shape conceptualizations of ethnicity in Turkey. The first is the tendency for individual rural villages to be inhabited by members of a group that shares a single language and religion and tends to be endogamic (marrying only within the village, or with nearby villages that share the same characteristics). Even today, traveling in rural Anatolia, one may pass in succession through a village that is Turkish-speaking and Sunni Muslim, a village that is Turkish-speaking and Alevi, a village that is Alevi and Zazaki-speaking (a language of the Northwestern Iranian language family related to the Kurdish languages), and so on. Some Turkish villages employ even more specific ethnic distinctions, such as Abdal, Avşar, or Yörük—all historical Turkish-speaking tribes. European sociologist Peter Andrews, in his pioneering book *Ethnic Groups in the Republic of Turkey* (1989), determined that modern Turkey featured forty-six distinct ethnicities.

The second factor that contributes to the nature of ethnicity within modern Turkey is the Ottoman Empire's policy of separating city neighborhoods by religious denomination. In Istanbul and other cities, some neighborhoods were officially designated as Jewish, Armenian Orthodox, Greek Orthodox, or Syriac Christian—ethnicities that continue to be officially recognized by the Turkish government. However, the state does not recognize Alevism, Kurdishness, or other tribal affiliations as official ethnicities, regarding their members instead as Turkish Muslims. For some Turkish citizens who grew up in an Alevi, Kurdish, or similar household, this official designation does not pose a problem. However, during the instances when Turkish-, Kurdish-, and Zazaki-speaking Alevis are persecuted for their way of life or beliefs, Alevism as a distinct ethnicity is most emphasized and becomes a politicized issue (Sökefeld 2008; van Bruinessen 1996).

Alevism is not just a religion or a set of beliefs but rather "a culture that shapes everyday life" (Ulaş Özdemir, quoted in Göktürk 2009). Central to Alevi culture is social music making, which always happens with the accompaniment of a *saz*-family instrument—indeed, the *saz* is regarded as sacred by Alevis. Two terms that refer to the social nature of music making, *muhabbet* and *hasbıhâl*, appear often in song, and *hasbıhâl* is so integral to Alevi musical life that the prominent spiritual leader and poet Dertli Divani (b. 1962) named his touring music ensemble the Hasbıhâl Topluluğu (Figure 1.2). *Muhabbet* and *hasbıhâl* both mean "conversation" but in the context of Alevi culture refer to gatherings where conversation happens through song, and in song lyrics *muhabbet* means "love." Rather than a strict performance, where there is a separation between a spatially demarcated performer and an audience, *muhabbet*-s often happen in people's homes. At a *muhabbet*, the *saz* is passed around the room so that many voices are heard, including musicians of all skill levels. Sabahat Akkiraz (b. 1955), perhaps the best-known female Alevi singer today, emphasizes that it was in *muhabbet* that she learned what she knows about Alevi music today. Her birth house was a place where most of the great twentieth-century Alevi *âşık* poets frequently came to participate in *muhabbet*.

> *Muhabbet*, in Alevi culture, includes the *saz* and the lyrics; it brings people together and expresses strong ties and spiritual meetings. In *muhabbet* everyone is accepted and everyone is equal. (Ulaş Özdemir, in Onat 2008)

The other primary contexts for Alevi music are *cem* ceremonies held in *cemevi*-s. Like *muhabbet*, *cem* music making is intended to bring

FIGURE 1.2 *A staged dance based on the* semah *tradition. Dertli Divani and the Hasbıhâl Topluluğu are performing different* saz-*family instruments.* *(Courtesy of the Kalan Müzik Archive)*

people together, but there are several key differences. First, traditional *cem* ceremonies were thought of as having a legal function, where the *dede* (religious leader) used song to mediate disputes between individuals or families. In much *cem* music, the lyrics are "challenges" directed to the listener to live a morally and ethically sound life. The *deyiş türküsü* "Zamanı Gelir," written by Âşık Mahrumi (1932–2006) and sung by Dertli Divani (CD track 5), epitomizes this challenge:

Üzülmeyin sonu ne olur diye	*Do not worry what will happen in the end*
Hesap sorulmanın zamanı gelir	*The time is coming for you to account for your deeds*
Bilmem bu ayrılık gayrilik niye	*I don't know why these differences and impossibilities exist*
Sıkı sarılmanın zamanı gelir	*It comes time to hug (each other) tight*

Another element of *cem* ceremonies that brings communities together is *semah*, a form of ritual dance with flowing circular movements done by men and women together (Figure 1.2). (For more information on *semah* music, see the multimedia materials on the book website, and Markoff 1986b and 2002a). While music for *semah* is strictly sacred repertoire and until very recently was only performed within a ritual context, other *cemevi* and *muhabbet* music is both sacred and secular, or, perhaps, ambiguous with regards to its sacred or secular function. Today in Istanbul, some *türkü* bars cater to Alevi clientele, performing *deyiş* and other *muhabbet* music genres in an obviously nonsacred context. Even contemporary rock and electronica groups perform Alevi repertoire: Sabahat Akkiraz sang on an album by the electronica act Orient Expressions, and the famed rock star Cem Karaca (1945–2004) created psychedelic rock covers of Alevi sacred and secular music repertoire.

ACTIVITY 1.2 *Listen to "Kalktı Göç Eyledi" (CD track 1), a bozlak sung by Alevi âşık Muharrem Ertaş, then to "Dadaloğlu," the cover by Cem Karaca (CD track 6). Besides the lyrics, what aspects of the two recordings are similar? Listen for musical instruments, singing style, and the occurrence of strong contrasts in musical texture.*

Alevi musician and ethnomusicologist Ulaş Özdemir (Figure 1.3) was born in Maraş in southeastern Turkey in 1976. His father, an architect, was a passionate music lover, and there was always Alevi and *âşık* music playing in the house. One picture taken of Ulaş when he was only two years old shows him holding a *saz*. Although Ulaş didn't have a long-term formal teacher, he learned much about Alevi music from sitting with *âşık* poets and *dede*-s (Alevi religious leaders) and from growing up in the local *cemevi* and *muhabbet* culture. Later, as an ethnomusicology student, Ulaş did field research with his father in the Maraş area, amassing a recorded archive of over one thousand songs. He also traveled to Iran to study the musical traditions of the Ah-le Haqq, Kurds with religious rituals and a music culture that has much in common with Turkish Alevism. He mainly performs traditional Alevi music and is well known for his performances with Dertli Divani and the Hasbıhâl Topluluğu.

Yet, Ulaş is also very connected to the contemporary music industry, as he was formerly the artist manager of Kalan Müzik (Turkey's largest independent record label). His musical interests extend to a love of Bob Dylan, Leonard Cohen, Nick Cave, and Tom Waits (whom he calls a "space poet" and sees as parallel to some Anatolian folk poets).

On the song "Âşık Oldur" (CD track 7) Ulaş performs the *dedesaz* and the *ruzba* (Figure 1.3), a kind of *cura* that once was common in

FIGURE 1.3 *Ulaş Özdemir and the* ruzba. *(Photo by Baran Özdemir, courtesy of the Kalan Müzik Archive)*

Alevi villages but now has almost entirely disappeared (see below for a detailed look at this instrument family). It is possible that Ulaş is the last living performer of the *ruzba*, and the instrument he plays on this song is over eighty years old. However, he stresses that this is not an "archeological" recording. For him, "music and culture are living and dynamic, not static" (Onat 2008). In "Âşık Oldur" and the other songs on the album *Bu Dem*, Ulaş hoped to capture the sense of *muhabbet*: "The 'dem' in the album's name, it means the now, it means this *muhabbet*, it expresses the emotions that I'm feeling" (ibid).

Although Alevi music is now known outside of Alevi traditional religious contexts, the sacred repertoire is not considered to be folk music, and little repertoire is included in the official government *türkü* archives. Yet, Alevi music is not clearly known as art or popular music, either. Alevi music lyrics are authored, and the culture takes pride in its poets and in the attribution of songs to the original poet. This has caused significant tension when popular performers cover Alevi songs on TV but do not give attribution. In the words of Dertli Divani:

> On television a man comes to center stage proclaiming "I'm an artist," and even though he is asked whose work he sang, he won't say. Even if he *wasn't* asked he *must* say. This work could belong to me or to another [Alevi] poet friend. Would it be so hard to mention this poet's name? If you won't say [who the real author is], why are you singing his songs? (Kalayacıoğlu and Öney 2007)

This concern with authorship is simply not found in the world of *türkü* singing, where authorship and composing new works is not a significant part of the present musical culture.

1.4 *SAZ*-FAMILY INSTRUMENTS

You have already encountered the long-necked lute known as the *saz* in relation to *âşık* and Alevi culture. The *saz* is found in many other musical practices as well, particularly as an accompaniment to *türkü* singing and several Central and Eastern Anatolian dance forms. Two interchangeable terms—*saz* (literally, "instrument") and *bağlama* (from the verb *bağlamak*, "to tie")—refer categorically to the members of one particular long-necked lute family. There are dozens of different named *saz* varieties (much like the violin, viola, cello, and bass in the violin family), ranging from the relatively short *cura* (about two and a half feet long) to the *divan* (five or more feet long) (Figure 1.4). The main measurement that distinguishes

FIGURE 1.4   *The* cura *(bottom),* tambura, *and* çöğür *(top).*   *(Instruments courtesy of Mustafa Avcı, photo by Ladi Dell'aira)*

TABLE 1.1   Saz-*family instruments by size and cultural features*

Name	Tekne Length	Cultural Features
cura	8-12″	Important for performing Alevi sacred and secular repertoire
dedesaz	12-14″	Main instrument for Alevi *cemevi* (sacred) repertoire
tambura	14-17″	Most ubiquitous saz, often called *bağlama*
çöğür	17-18.5″	Historically used for Abdal *aşık* repertoire (also called Abdal)
divan	>18.5″	Specific to Central Anatolia and inland Western Anatolia

different *saz* is the length of the *tekne*, the face from the edge of the bowl to the beginning of the neck (Table 1.1). The most ubiquitous *saz*, known as *tambura*, has a *tekne* ranging from fourteen to seventeen inches and, depending on the neck, can range from three to four feet in total length. However, different *saz*-family instruments are distinguished not only by size but also by repertoire and cultural associations.

ACTIVITY 1.3 *"Zamanı Gelir" (CD track 5) features several different* saz-*family instruments, including* bağlama, cura, dedesaz, *and* çöğür. *This song is arranged in sections featuring different combinations of one to four instruments at a time. Listen to discern where each new section begins and how many instruments are played in each section. Describe what makes you hear the number of instruments that you identify.*

S*az*-family instruments have three to eight strings arranged into three "courses." When there are more than three strings, two or three strings are grouped together into a course and tuned to the same note or to octaves in order to provide a louder sound and longer sustain. All *saz*-s use movable frets that are tied around the neck, so that the performer can choose which intervals to use. Typically, more frets are used for long-necked *tambura, çöğür,* and *divan* instruments, but tuning has become somewhat standardized, so that any two *saz*-s can usually be played in tune with each other. *Saz*-s are either played with a one-inch-long flexible pick known as a *tezene,* or with the fingertips or fingernails (a family of techniques collectively known as *şelpe*).

ACTIVITY 1.4 *Become familiar with the different playing styles by comparing the* tezene *style of "Karyolamın Demiri" (CD track 2) with the fingertip* şelpe *style of "Ey Zahit Şaraba" (CD track 8) and the fingernail* şelpe *style of "Âşık Oldur" (CD track 7).*

Due to the range of playing techniques and the versatility of the instrument in playing harmonic and melodic passages, the *saz* is used in a wide variety of musical styles. In some, the *saz* creates a monophonic single melody (CD track 3). In others, a *saz* produces a polyphony of multiple melodies and a complex harmonic structure (CD tracks 7, 8).

The *saz* often accompanies singing but also is used in dance music, particularly the Central Anatolian *misket* and the Aegean *zeybek* dances (see Section 7) (CD tracks 2, 30). Students of the *saz* today learn between ten and thirteen codified *saz* styles, each named after a region and discrete repertoire of music (Table 1.2). Two other named styles are sometimes mentioned, but not regionally defined: *karşılama*, a dance; and *deyiş/semah*, poetic forms and religious music of the Alevis. Each of these styles features a standard right-hand picking or strumming technique used only in that style.

This concept of regional style is recent; it is a result of national folklore projects that began in the 1920s and the TRT (Turkish Radio and Television) broadcasts of government-sponsored folk-music ensembles that launched in the late 1930s (Markoff 2002b). Before, most folk music was local, and though there were traveling musicians, there was not a widespread awareness of musical commonalities between the music of different villages.

TABLE 1.2 *Regional* saz-*playing styles as taught in* dershane *today*

Saz Style	Region or Cultural Delimiter
Eğe/Zeybek	The Aegean Coast and coastal mountain areas; *zeybek* dance
Silifke	The Mediterranean Coast and coastal mountain areas; spoon dances
Kayseri	Central Anatolia; Abdal Turkic music
Kırşehir/*bozlak*	Central-Eastern Anatolia; Abdal Turkic music, and the *bozlak* genre
Ankara	Central Anatolia; *misket* dance
Azeri	Azerbaijan and culturally Azeri places in Eastern Anatolia
Konya	Inland Western Anatolia
Yozgat/Sürmeli	Central Anatolia
aşıklama	Eastern Anatolian style of the *aşık* bards (particularly in Van and Kars)
Karadeniz	Black Sea coast
Trakya/Rumeli	European continental Turkey west of Istanbul
Teke	Burdur-Muğla region of Southwestern Anatolia; Yörük music
Kütahya	Inland Aegean Coast regional music

Since the 1960s, this sense of region has been amplified through two major nongovernmental pedagogical institutions: the *dernek* (club) and *dershane* (lesson house). Most urban *saz* players today attended one or more *dernek* or *dershane*, where they learned remote village repertoires in the convenience of an urban setting through group lessons with famous musicians. Teaching the music of thousands of Anatolian localities is an impossible task, but instruction in thirteen regional styles is feasible, and thus the idea of regionalism has become standardized and institutionalized.

To be a professional *saz* player today means having the skill to perform songs and improvisations in most of the regionally delimited styles. However, for each named style there are many local variants, and the better professional *saz* players work towards proficiency in performing songs in a locally appropriate manner, particularly that specific to their own family's ancestral village. Instead of learning this at a *dershane*, some *saz* players spend months or years living in a town or village studying the local playing style and repertoire, attaining an "authentic" feeling from immersion. Village immersion is a pedagogical method thought to be similar to how *saz* was traditionally taught. Irene Markoff noted this among the younger generation of Alevi *saz* artists in the 1970s–1980s (1990, 135). Many of these musicians today direct their own *dershane*, and their most serious students, on graduating, continue to practice this form of deep immersion.

The *saz*, more than any other melodic folk instrument, has been depicted through national broadcasts and government-sponsored concerts as the instrument played across the nation, even by all Turkic peoples in Central Asia. The *saz* has often been called the "national" instrument of Turkey, partly due to Atatürk's championing of the instrument in the 1920s–1930s and partly due to its ubiquitousness in government ensembles, although it has never officially held that designation. Turkish government folk-music orchestras, since the "Yurttan Sesler" (sounds of the homeland) radio program first aired in 1936, have always featured an ensemble foregrounding *saz*-family instruments (Markoff 1986a, 36–37). Today *saz* is played across the country, even in regions such as the Eastern Black Sea, where once it did not exist. Due to the systematic approach to teaching regional playing styles, *saz* players today learn an easy system for adapting folk melodies from any instrument to the *saz*.

1.5 *SAZ* MAKING

Long-necked lutes existed in Mesopotamia since Sumerian times—an engraving depicting a two-stringed lute was found in the royal tombs of Ur (2600 BCE)—and probably were widespread in Anatolia prior to the beginning of Turkic settlements in the eleventh century. However, the origin myths of the *saz* always focus on Central Asia. It is likely that the first Oghuz Turkic settlers in Anatolia brought long-necked lutes with them when they migrated from Central Asia starting in the eleventh century. The Kyrgyz *kopuz* is widely believed to be the original *saz*, and a derivative of it is still played in Kyrgyzstan.

Ottoman-era *saz*-s in Anatolia were most often made out of a single, carved piece of mulberry or chestnut wood, covered with a Sitka spruce face, to which was attached a straight neck carved out of hornbeam wood (Figure 1.5). However, according to Istanbul-based luthier Özbek Uçar, in those villages without chestnut and mulberry trees, local instrument makers improvised with other locally available hard fruitwoods or juniper for the body and neck, and with fir, pine, or other softwoods for the face. Anatolian-produced *saz*-s differed from Central Asian *kopuz*-s, as the same trees did not grow in both locations,

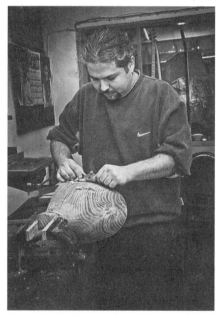

FIGURE 1.5 *Özbek Uçar carving a* bağlama. *(Photo by Ladi Dell'aira)*

and only recently has there been a system for transporting wood long distances.

Ecology and economics continue to impact *saz* making. Due to scarcity, it is now illegal to cut chestnut trees, and therefore makers are dependent on the infrequent occasions when the government cuts trees and makes wood available to luthiers for purchase. The availability of Sitka spruce also ebbs and flows, as the remaining spruce forests in the Black Sea are much smaller than they historically were. The market availability of African, Asian, and South American woods in the 1900s supplanted domestic efforts to create sustainable timber, so Turkey has not developed an extensive domestic hardwood forestry industry.

There is increased demand for quality instruments, locally and internationally, but traditional instrument-making techniques are not suited to mass production. Luthier Özbek Uçar continues to make instruments by hand and uses many traditional carving and wood-scraping tools. Working together, it takes three to five months, from start to finish, for Özbek, İlyas Demir, and İsmail Akpınar (the other two master craftsmen in his workshop) to make a single instrument. Their clientele consists mainly of professional Alevi performers, for whom they create truly custom instruments.

Another newer construction technique, modeled after oud making (see Chapter 2), replaces the carved bowl with one made of one-inch-wide wood staves glued together around a frame (Figure 1.6). This technique is quicker, uses considerably less wood, and allows the use of hardwoods that would be difficult to carve. In fact, many *saz* players now request wenge, rosewood, zebrawood, and other exotic African hardwoods, partly for the visual aesthetic and partly since such woods produce louder instruments. In the last couple of decades, some *saz*-s have even been stained flashy colors such as purple, red, and orange, or airbrushed with contemporary motifs. On the other hand, many professional Alevi musicians insist on nonstained carved-bowl instruments of chestnut or mulberry, because of their traditional significance as well as their distinctive, Anatolian sound quality. The iconic pictures of sixteenth-century folk poet Pir Sultan Abdal holding a carved-body *cura* above his head helps to instill the sense to which the unadorned carved *cura* is symbolic of Alevi identity itself.

An alternative production mode has emerged that allows for far greater numbers while preserving aspects of traditional luthiery. Hasan Sarıkaya, proprietor of Saz Müzik Aletleri, learned *saz* making from his

FIGURE 1.6 *Partially completed staved* bağlama *back and single detached stave.* *(Photo by Ladi Dell'aira)*

father, who in turn had learned while apprenticing for small luthier guilds in Istanbul. His factory, located in the Sarıgazi city just east of Istanbul, employs fifteen experienced instrument craftsmen and produces up to 250 instruments per month, many of which are exported to Turkish diasporic communities in Germany and elsewhere. When I visited the factory, Hasan led me through rooms filled with partly finished instruments—over ten thousand *saz*-s of different sizes in differing states of completion (Figure 1.7). The term "factory" (*fabrika*) is a bit of a misnomer—his instruments are built by master craftsmen, using a few semiautomated processes but still essentially by hand (Figure 1.8). However, Hasan plans to create a multilingual Internet-based ordering system, so that future customers can choose custom woods, instrument sizes, construction techniques, and ornamental details through convenient drag-down menus. His business has been influenced by contemporary production and distribution systems developed for the technology sector.

FIGURE 1.7 *In Hasan Sarıkaya's factory, instruments are stored in an unfinished state for several months in a multitude of rooms with different temperatures and humidities so that, when finished, they are less affected by changes in weather.* *(Photo by Ladi Dell'aira)*

FIGURE 1.8 *Craftsman planing a saz face in Hasan's factory, Saz Müzik Aletleri.* *(Photo by Ladi Dell'aira)*

1.6 *KEMENÇE* AND KARADENIZ FOLK SONG

While *saz*-family instruments are found throughout Anatolia and Central Asia, other rural music instruments are only found within a small region or locality and are only used for performing particular musical repertoires. The modern term *kemençe* refers to two very different bowed fiddles, each of which historically had a different name. The *Karadeniz kemençe* (hereafter referred to as *kemençe*; see Figure 1.9) is a small box fiddle that was historically played by and for Pontic Greek, Laz, and Turkish sailors, fishermen, and farmers who lived in modern-

FIGURE 1.9 *İlknur Yakupoğlu performing* kemençe *(CD track 9). İlknur was born in 1968 in Tonya, a rural district of the Trabzon Province, and like many children at the time learned to play* bağlama. *After moving to Ankara and performing in a government folk-music ensemble, she became curious about female* kemençeci *(*kemençe *performers) and conducted field research in Tonya. Through studies with both male and female* kemençeci *she found that the* kemençe *was, and still is, actively performed by women, despite mainstream perception to the contrary. İlknur performs solo and as a guest artist with the large fusion ensembles Kardeş Türküler and Grup Helesa. (Photo by Yeliz Keskin)*

day Turkey and Georgia and on the Black Sea's islands. The Laz ethnicity has lived in a small geographical area of coastal modern-day Turkey and Georgia at least since the Kingdom of Colchis ruled the region in the sixth century BCE. The Lazuri language is in the South Caucasian language family and related to Mingrelian and Georgian but not to Turkish or other Anatolian languages. The Laz converted to Sunni Islam during the Ottoman Empire period of rule. Due to mandatory Turkish-language education in the Turkish Republic, few Laz children grow up with fluency in the language, and even though there are probably several hundred thousand Laz living in the Karadeniz (Eastern Black Sea), perhaps only a few tens of thousands continue to actively speak the language.

> The fiddle culture of the Black Sea coast is linked, then, with that of Caucasian and Central Asian peoples, some Turkic, some not. The carriage of the kemençe to certain of the Greek islands by migrants from the Black Sea coast in 1922, and its spread and increase in importance in the new environment, is evidence of the long-standing association between the population of the Black Sea coast and the kemençe and of the cultural vigour of this hybrid population with its ancient Byzantine, Lâz and Turkish elements. (Picken 1975, 337)

Laurence Picken's description of the "Black Sea fiddle culture," based on research he conducted in the 1950s, emphasized hybridity and multiculturalism, but the modern-day Karadeniz is a different place. Today, the region is one of the most conservative and staunchly Turkish-nationalist regions in the whole country (with the exception of the coastal town Hopa), and despite the ample historical evidence to the contrary, the *kemençe* is proudly claimed by many to be a thoroughly Turkish instrument of Central Asian origin. Many Laz continue to live in the Karadeniz region, and although many enthusiastically joined the Turkish nationalist movement, over the last fifteen years there has been a Laz ethnic revival of sorts, and Lazuri-language recordings have begun to appear in the marketplace. Almost all professional *kemençeci*-s today are ethnically Laz, although not all would self-identify as such.

Until the twentieth century there was only one city in the Karadeniz—the ancient city of Trabzon—and the primary traditional occupation of the Black Sea coastal region was fishing. After World War II, the Black Sea became the site of state-controlled hazelnut and tea cultivation, producing all the tea and hazelnuts consumed in Turkey. Many songs

accompanied by *kemençe* sing of tea harvesting and of the mountain pla-
teaus above Rize, a popular site for summer festivals featuring *kemençe*
playing and *horon* dancing (see next section).

In contrast with *saz*-family instruments, which are now performed
in nearly every region of Turkey, the *kemençe* is only found in the narrow coastal strip of the Eastern Black Sea, extending from Giresun east
to the Georgian border, and in communities of immigrants from that
region (Pontic Greeks in Bulgaria perform an identical instrument
they call *Pontos lyra*, but there is little active connection between contemporary Anatolian and Bulgarian fiddle cultures). In governmental
folk-music ensembles, while the *saz* is used for performing music from
every region, *kemençe* is only used to play *türkü*-s and dance pieces from
the Karadeniz. The most characteristic aspects of the *kemençe* are the
incredible speed of song melodies and ornaments, with many *horon* line
dances exceeding 280 pulses per minute, and the playing of melodies in
parallel fourths.

1.7 DANCE MUSIC AND DRUMMING: *OYUN HAVASI* AND THE *ASKI-DAVUL*

*In traditional times, people danced together in a line. Then, modernity came,
and couples began dancing face-to-face. Now, postmodernity has come, and
people dance all by themselves.*

(Kudret Emiroğlu, December 7, 2006, Forty-fifth annual meeting of
the Middle East Technical University Folklore Club)

Kudret Emiroğlu, a cultural historian of the Eastern Black Sea Region,
is alluding to the importance of the line dance—the most ubiquitous
dance form in Turkey, as well as west into Greece and the Balkans,
north into Georgia and Armenia, and south into Syria, Lebanon,
Israel, Palestine, and Jordan. There is a huge diversity of line dance
styles, as most localities have their own variants of dance types that
are regionally distributed (Figure 1.10). Perhaps the best known is
the Central and Eastern Anatolian *halay* dance, danced by Turks and
Kurds at weddings and festivals and in *türkü* bar (as described in the
chapter introduction). However, in other parts of rural Anatolia *halay*
dancing is not known. Where *kemençe* music is found, so are the many
horon dances. In the mountainous regions just south of the Eastern
Black Sea coast, the *bar* is predominant, while further to the west along
the Black Sea coast the *karşılama* dances involve couples or two lines

FIGURE 1.10 *Regional dance distribution in Turkey. While some dances are found in a single region (e.g.,* horon *in the Eastern Black Sea), other dances span several regions (the* halay *is found in Central, Eastern, and Southeastern Anatolia, and along the eastern Mediterranean coast).*

of people facing each other. The Aegean and Mediterranean coastal regions feature dances that strongly differ from the aforementioned line dances. The Antalya-Silifke area features *kaşık oyunları* (spoon dances) performed by several dancers in a line playing wooden yogurt spoons for rhythmic accompaniment, while the Aegean Region features the *zeybek*, a showy male dance done to dramatic, slow-tempo music. All of these are typically performed outdoors and, depending on the locality, may be danced by men and women together or, due to locally observed Islamic prohibitions on mixed-sex activities, in lines separated by gender.

In the same way that the term *saz* refers to dozens of related yet different stringed instruments, *halay* and *horon* stand for dozens or hundreds of different dance varieties. The *hamsi horonu* ("anchovy line dance") is named after the most important fish in the Black Sea (and the most distinctive ingredient in Karadeniz coastal cuisine), and the fast-paced dance imitates the wiggling motion of anchovies right after they have been caught. Other *horon* varieties include the *düz horon* ("straight" dance) (Figure 1.11), the best-known variety and one done by people of all ages; the *deli horon* ("crazy" dance), which has sudden shifts from a subtle walk to jumps and shaking that happen while running; and the *dik horon* ("perpendicular" or "steep" dance), which involves complex footwork but less movement through space than the other styles. All

FIGURE 1.11   *Grup Helesa dancing a* horon *at the end of one of their concerts. Leading the line dance, on the left, is Ayşenur Kolivar (b. 1976 in Çayeli in the Rize Province), the director of Helesa and one of the most prolific ethnomusicologists doing field recordings of women's and men's songs in the Eastern Black Sea. She was the first singer to bring a style that clearly originated in Black Sea–village female singing traditions to the recording studio and stage (CD track 10).*   (Photo by Yeliz Keskin)

horon dances are characterized by the fast speed and two primary steps that alternate between the dancer being balanced and off-balance (see Chapter 3 and the concept of *aksak*).

If dances could have opposites, the *zeybek* would be the opposite of the *horon*. Whereas the speed of *horon* varieties ranges from 260 beats per minute to upwards of 300 beats per minute, a *zeybek* might be as slow as 40 beats per minute, slower than the pace of the human heartbeat. *Zeybek* dance involves dramatic movements contrasting with a variety of still poses, with the dancer standing either on one leg with his other leg raised in the air, or on one knee with both arms raised to the sky. In some localities, *zeybek* dancers circle a *rakı* glass placed on the floor, moving slowly closer to it. The *zeybek*, besides referring to a dance style, is a term for the outlaw soldiers who lived in the Aegean mountains and fought against Ottoman oppression of the region. In the 1920s *zeybek* soldiers joined the national army in enforcing the "population exchange" between Greece and Turkey and expelling the Armenian minority population of the area.

In most of Anatolia, the *askı-davul* (lit. "suspended drum") is the primary "dance drum." It accompanies stringed instruments in Aegean *zeybek*-s, it accompanies one or more *zurna* (double reeds) in Central, Eastern and Southeastern Anatolian *halay*-s, and it is part of the heterogeneous ensemble that is used to perform *karşılama* and other wedding dances in Thracian *Roman* villages. The one exception: it is only used for *horon* in the Trabzon city area, as most *horon*-s do not incorporate drums. The *askı-davul* is double-headed and played with one stick and one wooden mallet. The mallet produces two sounds: a loud and deep *düm* (bass drum sound), and a sharp, high-pitched accent made by striking the wooden drum frame. The footlong stick is held so that its entire length makes contact with the drum skin, resulting in a high-pitched sound named *tek* that is reminiscent of a snare drum. One of the markers of good *askı-davul* players, such as Ömer Avcı (CD tracks 2, 30), is the extraordinarily fast speed of their articulated stick rhythms.

ACTIVITY 1.5 *Many drums found throughout West and Central Asia, Southeastern Europe, and North Africa are similar to the Anatolian* askı–davul, *including the Bulgarian* tapan, *Armenian* dhol, *and Egyptian* tabl baladi. *However, there are differences in their sound and performance practice. Do a Web search to find similar drums in three additional countries, then look for information that compares and contrasts how they are played in each country.*

1.8 CONCLUSION: RURAL MUSIC IN URBAN TURKEY

Earlier, I mentioned the importance of government-sponsored national broadcasts of folk-music orchestras and educational institutions in creating a national consciousness about regional folk-music traditions. Since the 1960s another institution has had an immense impact on perceptions of rural music practices: the recording industry of Istanbul. Inside one six-story mall in the Unkapanı neighborhood, over one thousand privately owned music businesses operate, including record labels, promotion companies, wholesalers, media suppliers, and instrument stores. Some of the businesses specialize in regional folk-music styles, and local artists from rural Anatolia come to Unkapanı in order to "make the break" in the recording industry. The recordings produced in Istanbul are subsequently marketed to urban and rural consumers alike. The *horon* dance cassettes and CDs produced in Unkapanı have come to have a significant influence on local music practices in the Eastern Black Sea, just as the Alevi recordings made in Unkapanı are influential on Eastern Anatolian rural Alevi music making.

The most significant innovation due to broadcast and recordings has been the creation of regionally delimited aesthetic styles of music and dance. Prior to the 1950s no single *horon* or *karşılama* variety represented the entire Black Sea Region, but rather there existed hundreds of locally known styles with differing aesthetic features. In Istanbul today, one can go to a performance of Karadeniz music, meaning a show including songs from Trabzon, Rize, Hopa, and perhaps small mountain villages, supported by a heterogeneous musical group (rather than a solo instrument, as would have traditionally been the case). At these events only a small number of *horon* dance varieties are performed, and these few contemporary varieties sometimes mix and match from a number of local styles. While some of the diversity of styles has been lost, the regional cultural music and dance forms have a very strong vitality across Turkey and represent a way in which music and dance have been instrumental in creating a national consciousness about regional and local culture.

CHAPTER 2

Urban Musics and Instruments

The previous chapter explored musics with roots in rural Anatolian villages. This chapter focuses on urban art (*sanat*) and folk musics, especially on how these musics are performed and perceived today in Istanbul. Urban art music was profoundly impacted by the circulation of music and musicians between the Ottoman Empire cities of Istanbul, Bursa, Erzurum, Gaziantep, and Smyrna. Ottoman music, particularly the instrumental music repertoire, urban folk-dance rhythms, and numerous aspects of the melodic modal system known as *makam*, in turn transformed the urban musical practices of Egypt, Syria, Iraq, and the Balkans.

Two terms distinguish urban art music by language and historical period. *Klasik Türk Müziği* refers to the "classical" era of art music, during the rule of the Ottoman Empire (1299–1922), and includes instrumental works and songs in the Ottoman Turkish (Osmanlıca) language. *Türk Sanat Müziği,* today known by its acronym TSM, refers to contemporary art songs in the modern Turkish language, particularly those composed since the foundation of the Turkish Republic in 1923. In Section 1 I will explore these linguistic divisions as well as the broader history of urban art music.

As with rural musics, the primary art-music instruments are rich with complex meanings. In this chapter, I will compare three stringed instruments with contrasting cultural histories, associations, and musical repertoires. The oud is often perceived as a foreign or "ethnic" instrument, even though numerous notable Turkish performers have played it. In contrast, the *tanbur* is today regarded as a thoroughly indigenous art-music instrument and is only used in Klasik Türk Müziği and TSM performance. Ironically, until recently the *klasik kemençe* was not a classical instrument at all but rather a Greek folk instrument from the Aegean Region. It "became" classical through the pioneering recordings of Tanburi Cemil Bey (Section 9). Within a few decades, in the context of the urban art-music ensemble the *klasik kemençe* had all but replaced the violin, which itself had, several centuries ago, replaced indigenous fiddles. A central theme in this chapter is the changing nature of music pedagogy. During the Ottoman Empire, art music was neither a concert music nor taught through formal conservatories. Two of the traditional music-making environments—the Enderun school and Mevlevi Sufi lodges (Section 1)—no longer exist. People today experience art music through radio and TV, governmental institutions (conservatories, concert halls, and touristic sites), neighborhood associations known as *cemiyet*, and in restaurant-nightclubs. These new contexts have changed the repertoire performed and how audiences interact with musicians while experiencing performances. Also, audio recordings became uniquely important as pedagogical tools for urban art musics and have replaced other traditional, interpersonal, forms of music pedagogy.

Finally, in this chapter I discuss *Roman oyun havası*, one of the many urban folk-music styles that fall under the category of *Istanbul türküsü*. *Roman oyun havası* is a recently developed genre based on Aegean and Western Black Sea *karşılama* folk dances as interpreted and modified by the Rom "gypsies" who live and perform professionally in Istanbul. (Note: the terms *Rom* and *Roman* are not related to the Roman Empire or the Italian city but rather to the Romanes language spoken in many gypsy communities—see Seeman 2006). As many *Roman* musicians have mastered *Roman oyun havası*, art music, *and* popular song forms, and performances fluidly shift between genres, their performances raise complex questions about ethnicity and the extent to which categorizing music as "folk," "art," and "popular" ultimately makes sense in modern Turkey.

2.1 HISTORY OF URBAN ART MUSIC UNTIL 1950

The Anatolian-Mesopotamian region is home to some of the earliest well-documented art-music traditions. The ancient Greek philosopher Pythagoras's physics experiments led him to develop a music theory that today is still evident in Ottoman art music, and the tenth-century Persian philosopher al-Fârâbî's writings about musical modes and the power of music therapy are similarly relevant today. 'Abd al-Qâdir al-Mâraghî (d. 1435 in Herat) is considered the "father" proper of art music in Turkey, as he wrote a number of compositions that are still performed today, and penned insightful writings about the music of the time. Of the instruments he mentioned, the oud, *kanun*, and *ney* are still in use six hundred years later. By the sixteenth century, the heart of Ottoman cultural life moved to Istanbul, and a large repertoire of art music began to be created.

Klasik Türk Müziği, although often hastily described as a "court music," did not always receive direct patronage from the sultanate. It existed inside and outside the palace and was created by individuals representing a broad spectrum of society—slave musicians captured in Ottoman military conquests, merchants, bureaucrats, and Ottoman dignitaries themselves. Sultan Selim III, who ruled from 1789 to 1808, was a noted composer and invented over a dozen *makam*-s (musical modes). One center of Ottoman art music was the Enderun, an elite Christian boarding school that trained bureaucrats and dignitaries and offered courses in music, as well as in Persian and Arabic literature. It was believed that knowledge of the arts and literary sciences was essential for being an educated individual. The Enderun was important, not just for its pedagogical significance, but as a place where private performances of the best art music happened.

Many Ottoman-era singers and composers were devout Muslims of Persian or Turkish ancestry and trained as *müezzin* (orators of the call to prayer) or *hafız* (memorizers of the Qur'an). Consequently, there are parallels between the vocal technique used to produce Qur'anic recitation, the call to prayer, and art-music song. However, many famous instrumentalists and composers, particularly *tanbur* players, were ethnically Greek, Armenian, or Jewish (Feldman 1996, 48–49), and a large body of Ottoman art music was composed in the Hebrew language.

ACTIVITY 2.1 *Sultan Selim III was active not just as a composer but as a patron of art and architecture. Using online resources, research the artistic achievements of Selim III, and write a brief biography.*

The Mevlevi Sufi order, best known via the image of "whirling dervishes," grew in political and artistic importance from the 1500s through the early 1900s, and a considerable amount of music, sacred and secular, was created in the dervish lodges. Sufism is a form of Islamic mysticism that takes many forms around the world and typically features a strong emphasis on rituals including *zikr* (lit. "remembrance," a practice involving the intense, rhythmic recitation of the names of God) and *sema*, the whirling done by devotees known as "dervishes." Mevlevi *sema* is one of the most visually striking cultural practices in Turkey, as dervishes wear long white robes that fan out while they turn for a half hour or more in perfect circles, one hand raised towards God, the other pointed towards Earth. I mentioned *semah* in Chapter 1 when discussing Alevi *cemevi* ceremonies, and both Mevlevi *sema* and Alevi *semah* involve ritual circular movements done with musical accompaniment. However, in every other regard the two practices are different. In Alevi *semah*, men and women participate together in rituals (one form of *semah* is a couples dance), and *semah* provides key social functions that are part of the vitality and unity of Alevi villages. Mevlevi *sema* has a more clearly delineated class and status hierarchy between participants, is typically done by either men or women, and is more integrated with other forms of Islamic belief and ritual.

In Mevlevi Sufism, music is a significant part of both *zikr* and *sema*. As many composers of Mevlevi music also composed secular art music, Mevlevi sacred music is considered to be a form of Klasik Türk Müziği. The music for *sema* is a suite form known as *âyîn* (in track 11 you can hear Hafız Kâni Karaca singing an excerpt of a much longer *âyîn*) that does not overlap with other urban art musics, although the oud, *tanbur*, and *ney* are used in both secular art musics and *âyîn* (Figure 2.1). The *ney* end-blown flute has a special significance to Mevlevis, as Jalal ad-Din Rumi, the poet and spiritual founder of Mevlevism, played and wrote about *ney*. Many great art-music composers were practicing Sufis and, in addition to secular art songs, composed sacred *âyîn*-s.

While Klasik Türk Müziği is undeniably an indigenous creation, it was through contact with European musicians and foreign diplomats stationed in the Ottoman Empire that much of the history and knowledge of the repertoire was preserved. We know about the works of Ottoman composer Buhurizade İtri (d. 1711), for example, through the writings of the exiled Moldavian prince Dimitrie Cantemir (1673–1723), who studied *tanbur*, *makam*, and composition from them and wrote extensively about music in Istanbul life. Cantemir was the first to notate Ottoman art music, including works from his teachers as well as those by al-Mâraghî and other historical composers (Popescu-Judetz 1999). Later in the eighteenth century, French diplomat Charles Fonton studied *tanbur* and wrote several books praising the virtues of Turkish music, which made an impact in European literary circles of the time (Shiloah 1993).

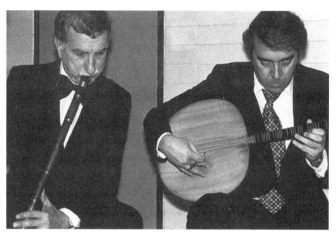

FIGURE 2.1 *Necdet Yaşar and Niyazi Sayın* tanbur–ney *duo. Note that most of the* tanbur *neck is not visible in this picture.* *(Courtesy of the Kalan Müzik Archive)*

Another form of foreign influence came through the introduction of European art music. In 1797, Sultan Selim III (1761–1808) brought an opera company to Istanbul for the first-ever staging of a full opera there, and by 1828 Giuseppe Donizetti (the brother of the Italian opera composer Gaetano Donizetti) was employed to assist with the creation of an Italian-style music conservatory in Istanbul. Around the same time, Hamamizade İsmail Dede Efendi (1778–1846) developed a compositional style and several new *makam*-s incorporating extensive melodic **modulation** (shifting between one melodic mode and another) (CD track 11). His style, inspired by European art music of the time, signified a change in musical aesthetics contemporaneous to the Romantic style of composition that was unfolding in Germany. Subsequent composers continued to be influenced by European musical trends and concepts of virtuosity.

Prior to Dede Efendi, art-song lyrics were sung in Osmanlıca (the Ottoman language). During the nineteenth century, an increasing number of *şarkı*-s (songs) were written in colloquial street Turkish, the predecessor to modern Turkish. The linguistic designation is significant: Osmanlıca was written in a modified Arabic script and had extensive loanwords from Arabic and Persian. The creation of modern Turkish was a monumental project spearheaded by Mustafa Kemal Atatürk, which began in 1928 with the conversion to an extended Latin script.

Through Atatürk's sponsorship, the newly formed Turkish Language Association researched the "true" roots of the Turkish language, creating a new language by subjecting Turkish to a "cleansing" process whereby Arabic and Persian influences were removed (Lewis 1999). In some cases, new words were fabricated based on Turkish roots (e.g., *bilgisayar*, lit. "knowledge enumerator," the term for computer). Sometimes scholars reintroduced ancient Turkic words that had not been spoken in centuries. When no suitable Turkish term existed, French terms were often incorporated (e.g., *lise*, "school," from *lycée*). The project was highly successful—modern-Turkish speakers without schooling in Osmanlıca may understand very little of the meaning of Klasik Türk Müziği song lyrics. This linguistic split precipitated the need to differentiate between Klasik Türk Müziği and TSM.

Several major historical events greatly impacted the vitality of Ottoman- and Turkish-language urban art musics. Following Sultan Selim III's death in 1808, court support for art music began to decline, leaving the Mevlevi Sufi dervish lodges as a primary context for art music. In 1925, by government decree, all Sufi lodges were closed and the public performance of Ottoman art music was banned. The music ban was relaxed a few years later, but the Sufi lodges remained closed for several decades. More than just economics, the legal action against Ottoman art music had a deep psychological impact on public perception. Rather than being seen as a rich and vibrant part of Turkish cultural history, urban art music became perceived as a multicultural (in other words, not purely Turkish), archaic, and elitist institution. When Sufi lodges reopened starting in the late 1990s, they no longer functioned as primary spaces for urban art-music performance. If you visit Turkey today, you typically will encounter "whirling dervish" performances in historic Sufi lodges, which are spectacles staged for tourists rather than religious rituals integral to the ongoing cultural practice of Mevlevi Sufis (Vicente 2007).

Starting in the 1950s, the government began increased support of urban art music through the creation of radio orchestras and regular radio broadcasts. A particular focus was on TSM (Türk Sanat Müziği), particularly Turkish-language şarkı-s (songs) that had been written in the late Ottoman or early Republican era (roughly 1828–1950). In contrast to the music's traditional small-ensemble aesthetic, new government-sponsored performances and radio broadcasts involved large, heterogeneous ensembles of Turkish and Western art-music instruments (CD tracks 12, 13). Although the music was broadcast all over Turkey, şarkı singing continued to be primarily an urban phenomenon.

Ensemble performances happen today in Turkey's larger cities, particularly in Istanbul, Ankara, and Izmir, and a number of universities in Turkey offer undergraduate and doctorate degrees in *sanat* (art) music. However, as I will show later in this chapter, it is possibly in the context of the *cemiyet*-s (music associations) and *meyhane*-s (restaurant-nightclubs) that the music today sees its liveliest performances.

2.2 OUD

The oud (sometimes written as *'ûd* in modern Turkish) is not considered a native instrument to Turkey or to Turkic peoples, although it has been played in Anatolia for at least five centuries. Instruments similar in shape and size to the modern oud existed in Baghdad since the sixth century, and the instrument became central to both Arab and Persian musics before being brought to Anatolia. However, the oud was a major instrument in the sixteenth-century Ottoman courts and has since become associated with a variety of social and ethnic identities. Today, within Turkey the oud is an important part of art-music (*klasik* and TSM) ensembles, urban *fasıl* orchestras, and *Roman* dance bands (see below), and it is featured in *arabesk* popular music, TV-show soundtracks (see Chapter 4), and Kurdish urban folk and popular music. Istanbul is widely regarded as the current capital of oud construction, and musicians from all over the world come to Turkey to purchase custom high-quality instruments.

The modern oud in Turkey has eleven strings, organized in five double-courses with a sixth, single bass string. The oud neck is fretless, like a violin neck, allowing any intervals or microtones to be performed with ease. The oud is played with a long, slender pick that traditionally was made of an eagle's quill but today is fashioned out of molded plastic. One of the most striking visual characteristics of the modern oud is the striped bowl pattern, a result of bending very thin (approximately $\frac{3}{32}$" thick) staves of wood over a mold. This staved construction, first developed by oud-making luthiers, has since been incorporated in other instruments, including the Greek *bouzouki*, the *saz*, the European lute, and the *tanbur*. A variety of woods, ranging from indigenous fruit-woods (mulberry, walnut, and pear) to exotic hardwoods (ebony, rosewood, and wenge) can be coaxed into bending into the proper shape, and little wood is wasted in the process.

Ramazan Calay (b. 1973) is a young oud maker whose workshop is located in the Kadıköy neighborhood of Istanbul (Figure 2.2). He

FIGURE 2.2 *Ramazan Calay finishing making a new oud.* *(Photo by Ladi Dell'aira)*

learned much of the trade through apprenticing with his uncle Mustafa Copçuoğlu (b. 1965), one of the foremost luthiers in Turkey. Ramazan has between two and four apprentices, who, like Ramazan fifteen years ago, have aspirations of becoming professional luthiers. Oud making has a long history of such apprenticeships, extending back to the Ottoman-era craft guilds that were centered in specific neighborhoods of historic Istanbul. Many of the ouds that Ramazan makes are faithful to the styles of the nineteenth-century Greek luthier Manol (Manolis Venios) and the twentieth-century Armenian luthier Onnik Karibyan, who both practiced their craft in Istanbul. However, Ramazan also experiments, using different woods for the face and body (including African woods such as those now used for *saz* making), and changing the shape of the fingerboard and the bracing system that holds the face onto the body of the oud. Like *saz*-craftsman Özbek Uçar, Ramazan exclusively makes custom instruments, creating approximately six new instruments a month.

Ramazan's shop is not just a place for luthier apprenticeship or commerce but a place for listening to serious Klasik Türk Müziği. At any time, up to ten musicians might be at Ramazan's shop, from twelve-year-old oud beginners to conservatory students and teachers to older amateur and professional musicians. This performance and learning environment is known as *meşk*, a term that describes music pedagogy during the Ottoman Empire, before conservatories and music schools were founded, where a group of musicians of all ages and skill levels passed instruments around a circle. In the case of Ramazan's shop, it is Ramazan's own custom-made ouds that are passed around, and in addition to commenting on the younger musicians' interpretations of classical music repertoire, elders comment on the tonal quality, the playability, and the visual aesthetics of the most recent creations, giving valuable feedback to Ramazan. I frequently went to Ramazan's shop, to get critical feedback on my own oud playing as well as to experience the range of sounds that could be produced with Ramazan's instruments.

In the same way that the *tanbur* recordings of Tanburi Cemil Bey (1875–1916) became the singular reference for later generations of *tanburi*-s, the oud recordings of Yorgo Bacanos (1900–1977) are intimately known by all oudists who perform art music (CD track 14). In my own lessons with Necati Çelik (Figures 2.3, 2.4), we often listened together to Yorgo's recordings, both to understand the art of *makam* and to scrutinize the way he interpreted melodies through ornamentation. Yorgo was ethnically Greek but fluent in Turkish and self-identified as

FIGURE 2.3 *Necati Çelik (second from left) learning oud through* meşk *from his teacher, Cinuçen Tanrıkorur (left, 1938–2000) and Hafız Kâni Karaca (second from right 1930–2004).* (Photo courtesy of Necati Çelik)

FIGURE 2.4   *Since the 1990s, Necati himself has become a prominent oud teacher in Istanbul, offering private and group (meşk-style) classes out of his office in the Kadıköy neighborhood, pictured above.   (Photo by Ladi Dell'aira)*

a citizen of Istanbul. His many innovations in playing technique helped make the oud an instrument capable of virtuosic performance.

Profile: I first met Necati Çelik (b. 1955) in 1993 when he toured in America with the Necdet Yaşar ensemble. I was amazed at the expressive power of his playing, the sheer variety of ornaments that he subtly used for interpreting melodies, and his explorations of improvisation in some of the more esoteric melodic modes found in Klasik Türk Müziği. It was his playing, in fact, that first inspired me to travel to Turkey to study oud and conduct research into the contemporary performance practice of urban art music. CD track 15, "Muhayyerkürdi Saz Semaisi," is an example of his unique ornamentation style. In addition to modernist interpretations of art music (which he does via solo concerts, small-ensemble performances, and his work with the

Istanbul State Turkish Music Ensemble; see Chapter 4), Necati also interprets the folk music of his native Konya (on both oud and *saz*) and is an active performer of Mevlevi *âyîn*.

2.3 CONTEXTS 1: EMİN ONGAN ÜSKÜDAR MUSİKİ CEMİYETİ

The term *meşk*, in Ramazan's oud shop or Necati's oud classes, refers to the learning and performance of art music in a group setting, with participants ranging in age and experience. Another kind of *meşk* exists in the context of neighborhood music schools known as *cemiyet*. The Emin Ongan Üsküdar Musiki Cemiyeti, which opened in 1918, is the oldest such school, famous for its one-hundred-year dedication to art-music performance and for its numerous members who went on to become famous performers and composers of art music. Composer and *cemiyet* teacher Cahit Deniz explained *meşk* to me as a kind of group learning—unlike private lessons or conservatory education—where students learn singing through aural skills and imitation rather than by reading musical scores. *Meşk* classes are a kinesthetic experience. Students tap out *usul* (metrical structures; see the next chapter) on their thighs while singing melodies using solfege syllables (do-re-mi). However, the *meşk* of the *cemiyet* is different than the *meşk* at Ramazan's workshop or the *meşk* of historical art-music pedagogy. Ottoman-era *meşk* was a group practice too, but the emphasis was on careful listening to and critique of individual performances by musicians of all levels, and thus structurally resembled Alevi *muhabbet* (Chapter 1).

At the *cemiyet* schools, the focus is on active participation and monophonic choral singing. A conductor conducts upwards of sixty choir singers and an orchestra with ten or more amateur performers of oud, *tanbur, kanun, klasik kemençe*, violin, *ney*, cello, and percussion. The Üsküdar Musiki Cemiyeti has several levels of classes and hosts hundreds of students at any given time. Although no formal degrees are given, students are motivated to work hard so they can take an exam at the end of the academic year; successful completion allows them to advance to the next level and attain more focused, private instruction on vocal styling and repertoire interpretation. Participants are typically not professional musicians, although many well-known twentieth-century musicians (including composer Selahattin Pınar, CD tracks 13, 16) taught or studied at Üsküdar.

Aslı Akoba has been a participant at the Üsküdar Musiki Cemiyeti for sixteen years. During her childhood, her mother and grandmother constantly listened to music on the radio at home, particularly the TRT (Turkish Radio and Television) classical station. Aslı also loves Western jazz music, but notably while living abroad she discovered how important Turkish-language *sanat* music was to her life. I interviewed Aslı about the social nature of music pedagogy at the *cemiyet*, about *meşk*, and about what *sanat* music means to her.

E: Obviously there's a social aspect to the *cemiyet* that people like, but why do people like the music making in the *cemiyet*? What attracts people to it, in your opinion?

A: Well, there are a couple of things. The school itself attracts people because it is the oldest *cemiyet* in Turkey, and the people who were here in the *cemiyet*, later on, formed the national radio, the *conservatoires*, the government choruses—like Nevzat Atlığ (CD track 12), so this is a very important place. So for whoever likes this type of music, it's a dream of theirs to spend time here. Even though there are exams, it's not hard to get in like the *conservatoires*, the national radio, or the government ensembles because there is no limit to the number of students accepted and you do not need to know many things about music to enter. Only an ear for music is needed. And this is like a hobby place—it's not your job. People who like Turkish classical music, who'd like to learn more and who'd like to be in a social environment, first they think of *cemiyet*. It's more disciplined, it's more serious. And you can see that you learn a lot. It's not just the singing, you learn the methods, you can observe others, it's also challenging, but attractive to be able to pass to a higher class.

E: How do you describe the kinds of music that you sing at the *cemiyet*, and what do these musics mean to you?

A: We do music from centuries ago, and very recently composed, even written a couple months ago. We're not doing religious music [i.e., Sufi music], even though it's all within each other [i.e., interrelated]. We're not doing political or any "taking sides" kind of music. We are all objective and all in the middle of everything. That's very important to us. I believe that's how we survived for ninety years and the others haven't.

E: Could you talk a little bit more about *meşk* as it's done at *cemiyet* and what the feeling or experience of *meşk* is like?

A: When I first got into the *cemiyet* we never had notes. They gave [them] to the instrument players only. They had us write and look

at the lyrics, and tap the *usul*. Just tap it and look at the lyrics, and
work on the same line, again and again, or the same measure again
and again until you become crazy! Then you started feeling why
you did it, because you understood it. Before there were notes,
people were only singing and tapping the *usul*, and that's how
they passed it on for years, from generation to generation. And
you never forgot the songs.

E: What does this music mean to you and how does it make you feel?

A: You have to have the rhythm, the *usul*, you have to tap the *usul* on
your knees. They first teach you that, so you realize the music you
thought was "in your genes" has a very important rhythm for your
soul and your body as well. Most of the songs, of course, talk about
love, separation, getting together, how you miss the one you love,
or death in wars or through illness, so you think you might want
to approach it like that, but then you feel the rhythm, you get to
know about the rhythm, you realize how important it is to calm
down and feel it, and then to perform. And then you realize it is
like a big ocean, that you're trying to survive in that water without
drowning! You have to be patient!

Then of course they teach you not to be loud. That's a very
important rule in Turkish singing. You have to be as silent, as calm
as possible, and you have to use your *kafa sesi* [a special kind of
head voice]. You have to have your voice go up to your brain and
come back! I don't know how else to describe it. So it comes from
inside you, it doesn't come from your throat. You might be doing it
already, but you don't know what you're doing. You start hearing
the difference... There are lots of people who have albums or [are]
on TV—you can tell who's doing it right or not.

2.4   *ŞARKI* AND *FASIL*: SONG AND
SUITE FORMS

The best-known and most ubiquitous urban art-song form, and the primary genre at the *cemiyet*, is *şarkı*. It was the first urban art-music form
to be sung in Turkish (instead of in Ottoman or Persian), and for literary
historians it is a "national genre that encapsulates the emotional life
of the Turks" (Klaser 2001, 3). Rajna Klaser describes the meaning of
şarkı, since the 1600s, as being about "imagining Istanbul as an earthly
paradise" (ibid, 219). *Şarkı* is related to urban and rural folk music, as
it uses Turkish folk poetic forms and rhythmic meters originating in
folk dance, but became an art music when composers incorporated the

influence of Persian poetic forms and the art-music *makam* modal system. According to historian Yılmaz Öztuna, this transformation happened at the same time, and in a similar manner, as the transformation of German folk song (*lied*) into the *lied* classical art-song form (exemplified by Franz Schubert and Robert Schumann's art songs) (ibid, 2). Although *şarkı*-s are usually in Turkish, the genre reflects the multicultural population of Istanbul, and many great *şarkı*-s were composed by Armenian, Greek, and Jewish composers, hailing from all social classes. Many *cemiyet* teachers themselves compose new *sanat* music repertoire, creating works that are added to the official government archive of art-music repertoire and often subsequently performed by government ensembles as well as by the *cemiyet*. Thus, the urban art-music tradition of *şarkı* singing lives on, not only through the performance of classic older compositions, but through the expansion of the repertoire in the form of new works that are very much in the "classic" style.

One important characteristic of urban art music is the performance of suites of works that relate through melodic mode and differ regarding musical meter and tempo. The *fasıl* is a suite that begins and ends with instrumental works, which frame a sequence of songs beginning with slower works and ending with faster, often better-known *şarkı*. The meaning of *fasıl* and the kinds of works performed have changed substantially. During the nineteenth century at the Enderun school, the *fasıl* art form involved the use of numerous song forms besides *şarkı*, some of which are scarcely known today. In contrast, during the same period, *fasıl* also referred to suites of pieces performed at *gazino* nightclubs in the Istanbul neighborhood of Pera (Beken 1998). As the clientele of the *gazino* was multiethnic, performers often sang the same repertoire in different languages (Greek, Turkish, and Armenian), depending on the composition of the audience. The nightclub context for *fasıl* has not disappeared, and *fasıl* performances that happen today at fancy *meyhane* restaurant-nightclubs (see Section 7) typically feature well-known sentimental love songs sung by a singer with very expressive gestures.

Star *fasıl* singers include both men and women, and due to the fact that the Turkish language is ungendered (the pronoun *o* means either "he" or "she"), any song can be sung by a man or a woman. However, *fasıl* performance often involves considerable gender ambiguity, particularly since many noted singers have been either transgender or, more recently, transsexual (an aspect shared with the *arabesk* popular-music genre; see Chapter 4). Zeki Müren (1931–1996), regarded as one of the great *fasıl* and TSM singers of the 1950s–1960s (CD track 16), became more conspicuously transgender later in his career, while Bülent Ersoy

(b. 1952) lived in exile outside of Istanbul for seven years following her sex-change operation. The pronounced sentimentality of the *fasıl* singing style, perhaps, is a natural complement to the gender ambiguities of some star performers.

2.5 *TANBUR*

Of all the instruments that are used today to perform urban art music, the long-necked *tanbur* (Figure 2.1) is arguably the "most classical" of all, as it is used almost exclusively for Klasik Türk Müziği and Mevlevi sacred music. The *tanbur* is a frail instrument, with a very thin fir-wood face and eight metal strings, arranged in three courses, strung along its four-foot-long neck. I recall two solo *tanbur* concerts when the face of the instrument caved in during the performance. On both occasions, the *tanburi* (*tanbur* player) had a spare instrument ready, suggesting that such accidents were not unexpected. This fragility, in part, lends the *tanbur* its unique sound (CD track 17). Even though several *tanbur* makers invented instruments that are structurally stronger, most *tanburi* prefer the original design. *Tanbur* makers have also not embraced exotic foreign woods or wild instrument colors in the way that oud and *saz* luthiers have facilitated aesthetic innovations. In construction, as well as in playing technique and repertoire, the *tanbur* has changed little.

Due to the *tanbur*'s very long neck, it is possible to fit many (movable) frets along the fingerboard. The art music performed on *tanbur* utilizes a *makam* (melodic modal) system with twenty-four named notes per octave, but in practice there are even more unique pitch classes (Signell 1977). Many contemporary performers tie thirty-six or more frets within the first octave of their instrument, which allow the playing of a wide variety of intervals that do not exist in any other musical system in the world. Moreover, the *tanbur* offers an obvious visualization of the tuning system for Turkish urban art music. It has been a key instrument for teaching the *makam* modal system itself since at least the eighteenth century, when European travelers Prince Cantemir and Charles Fonton learned to play *tanbur* with considerable skill (Feldman 1996).

Relatively recently, the Ottoman composer and multi-instrumentalist Tanburi Cemil Bey recorded more than one hundred wax cylinders and 78 rpm discs (O'Connell 2002). Of these, his improvisations on *tanbur* are regarded as among the most significant Ottoman-era art-music recordings and continue to be the most imitated *tanbur* recordings. Students of every instrument learn these improvisations by rote, using

FIGURE 2.5   *Tanburi Cemil Bey.*   *(Courtesy of the Kalan Müzik Archive)*

them as a guide to understanding the art of melodic improvisations in each unique *makam*. Although Cemil Bey (Figure 2.5) did not intend for his recordings to have a pedagogical function per se, through his work the *tanbur* continues to be a primary technology for teaching *makam*. Musician and music theory teacher Ahmet Erdoğdular encourages his students to learn *makam* and the art of improvisation by using computer software such as the Amazing Slow Downer to digitally "stretch" Cemil Bey recordings. In slow motion, the mechanics of melodic ornaments and the precise intonation of pitches can be more easily perceived. Computer-software manipulation of recordings is obviously a very recent possibility and might seem to be more in the domain of the work a recording engineer would do when producing pop music, but here it is used in the pursuit of learning historical art music.

2.6   INSTRUMENTAL ART-MUSIC COMPOSITION

One of the main repertoires for the *tanbur* is purely instrumental urban art music, consisting of three principal musical forms: the *saz semaisi*, the *peşrev*, and the *longa*. The primary difference between the three is in musical time (*usul*; see Chapter 3): *saz semaisi*-s are notated almost entirely in a slow $\frac{10}{8}$, *longa*-s are fast, dance-style pieces notated in $\frac{2}{4}$ or $\frac{6}{8}$, and *peşrev*-s are notated in a variety of long and complex musical meters. The forms also differ in where they occur in a musical performance; a *peşrev* always begins a suite of instrumental or vocal selections, while a *saz semaisi* or *longa* ends a suite.

All *saz semaisi*-s are named after the *makam* (musical mode) in which they are written, as in "Bestenigar Saz Semaisi" and "Mühayyerkürdi Saz Semaisi." Unlike in Classical-era European art music, where most compositions used either the major or minor mode, during the same period in Ottoman art music several hundred such modes were created. Just as late nineteenth-century European Romantic compositions exhibited increasing atonality and **chromaticism** in a shift from Classical conceptions of musical harmony, modernist *makam*-s display increasing chromaticism, a greater use of scalar melodic runs, and a larger ambitus (range between the highest and lowest notes of a piece) than classical ones.

ACTIVITY 2.2 *"Mühayyerkürdi Saz Semaisi" by Reşat Aysu (CD track 15) is an example of a "modernist" piece composed in 1967 in a relatively recently invented* makam. *Listen for the quick, scalar succession of notes in the first few seconds of the piece. This flashy display of virtuosity would not have been found in eighteenth-century compositions. Then, listen to "Bestenigar Saz Semaisi" (CD track 17), an eighteenth-century work by Tanburi Numan Ağa that corresponds to the "Classical" era of* Klasik Türk Müziği, *written in one of the oldest known* makam-s. *Compare the two with regards to the presence (or absence) of scalar melodic runs and chromaticism, as well as ambitus.*

2.7   *ROMAN OYUN HAVASI*

Roman oyun havası is a form of dance music that has been immensely popular in Istanbul since the 1960s. To understand this music, it is important to first discuss the Rom, an ethnicity commonly referred to as *çingene* ("gypsies"), who have lived in western Anatolia since the ninth century (*Rom* is the noun form, *Roman* the adjective form). The Rom of Istanbul have lived in the Gaziosmanpaşa and Sulukule neighborhoods for over five hundred years and have had a significant role in Istanbul's musical life for much of that time, particularly in art-music performance. The half-million Rom living in Turkey, along with the Muslim Rom in Southeastern Europe, comprise the Xoraxane *Roman* ethnicity. In addition to Turkish, many speak the Xoraxane dialect of the Romanes language.

The music now known as *Roman oyun havası* has its roots in an indigenous (although not ethnically *Roman*) folk dance called *karşılama*. According to ethnomusicologist Sonia Seeman (2002), *Roman* wedding dance bands in Keşan and other towns west of Istanbul along the Greek border started performing their own variants on this traditional music and dance form, which spread within Rom communities throughout western Anatolia. The Istanbul-centered recording industry subsequently marketed *Roman oyun havası* as an urban dance-music genre, and the popularity of this led *Roman* musicians to create new compositions and to abandon many other forms of music they had once played.

The primary stylistic traits that distinguish *Roman oyun havası* from other dance-music styles are the presence of clarinet as the lead melody instrument, and the dense, driving percussion rhythms in a fast $\frac{9}{8}$ meter played on the *askı-davul* and the *darbuka* (goblet-shaped drum). Track 18 is a characteristic *Roman oyun havası* performed by clarinetist Selim Sesler. The music, additionally, sometimes accompanies staged dance performances, which have become known in the West as "Turkish-style belly dance." The associations with this dance form, which is sexually much more provocative than is normally considered acceptable in a strongly Muslim society, have led many to regard *Roman oyun havası* itself as morally questionable. However, the music continues to be immensely popular across social classes in Istanbul and is a favorite style of social dance music for weddings and *meyhane* performances (see the next section). Ultimately, like many things in contemporary Istanbul, the Rom, and the dance musics that they perform, are regarded in an ambiguous and contradictory light by mainstream society.

2.8 CONTEXTS 2: RESTAURANT AND *MEYHANE* MUSIC

The *meyhane* is a restaurant-like place that serves alcohol and features live performance of *şarkı, fasıl, İstanbul türküsü* (CD track 19), and, less frequently, Aegean and Istanbul folk dances and the more "serious" strands of popular music. The *meyhane* is a direct descendent of the Ottoman-era *gazino* nightclub (which like the *meyhane* served alcohol) and the Janissary coffeehouse. Today's *meyhane* clientele are Turkish-speakers, and thus songs are only sung in Turkish (in contrast to the nineteenth-century *gazino*). However, the musicians may be Turks or may self-identify as members of other ethnicities. Many Rom perform in *meyhane*, although the music they perform in this context would be perceived as urban *sanat* or *halk* music (with no ethnic signifier) rather than as ethnically *Roman* music.

Meyhane performances typically consist of *fasıl* suites with a wide variety of TSM, *türkü*, and sometimes dance- or pop-music selections. Interestingly, I observed an increasing tendency for *Roman* musicians to perform elaborate arrangements of esoteric works from Klasik Türk Müziği instrumental repertoire, including many of the most difficult *peşrev*-s, *saz semaisi*-s, and *longa*-s. As this repertoire is widely perceived as being "serious" music with higher social-class associations, *Roman* musicians perhaps use these performances to assert a higher social class than might be assumed if they played only popular dance works. Inevitably, at some point the audience demands either well-known songs or dance numbers, and a more normative, interactive performance of TSM and dance music begins.

In the *meyhane* context, singing is an intensely participatory affair, as members of the audience write requests on napkins that are passed to the musicians, often dedicating particular songs to individuals or to whole tables. Everyone sings along, and the audience often overpowers the soloist in the *fasıl* orchestra. It is not uncommon for the same song to be requested two or more times during an evening, the idea being that the song takes on new meanings in light of the experiences that have transpired since it was last sung. In some *meyhane*-s, musicians alternate between upbeat dance pieces (*Roman oyun havası* or other folk dances) and slow, melancholy songs. This whole style of music making is so prevalent there is even a Turkish verb—*fasıl yapmak*—meaning "to do fasıl."

While *meyhane* repertoire consists primarily of urban music forms, in many ways the space is similar to the *türkü* bars discussed in Chapter 1. In both environments, audience participation is essential, including the ubiquitous request napkins, the sing-along, and members of the audience commandeering the microphone to sing a song. While *meyhane* are the favored nightclubs for Istanbul natives and other urbanites, *türkü* bars cater to Istanbul residents who culturally identify most with their rural *memleket* (ancestral birth-home). The two milieus also differ in terms of ensemble, with the *meyhane* featuring art-music instruments for the most part, and the *türkü* bar featuring one or more *saz*-family instruments, accompanied by other rural Anatolian instruments.

2.9 KLASIK KEMENÇE (LYRA POLİTİKİ)

One instrument in particular preserves a sense of what urban folk-dance music may have sounded like in Istanbul and Smyrna (modern-day Izmir) in the 1700s and 1800s: the *klasik kemençe*. At the time, the instrument was most commonly called by its Greek name, *politiki lyra* ("city fiddle"), and similar fiddles were used throughout the Aegean Region for performing men's *köçek* dances (Aksoy 2005, 9). Like the *Karadeniz kemençe* (Chapter 1), the *klasik kemençe* is a small three-stringed fiddle. Unlike its Eastern Black Sea cousin, the *klasik kemençe* is pear shaped (hence one of its other names—the *armut* ["pear"] fiddle). It is fingered with the backs of the fingernails, rather than with the fingertips as is common for violin-family instruments.

From the late 1800s through the early 1900s, the *politiki lyra* was not perceived as a high-class instrument nor used for art music, due to its popularity in *gazino*-s, its importance for folk dance, and its Greek cultural associations. So how did the *politiki lyra* replace the violin and become *the* classical fiddle of Turkey? The clue is found in the earliest surviving significant body of recordings made during the Ottoman era—the *klasik kemençe* solos of Tanburi Cemil Bey—which marked the transformation of a lower-social-class, nightclub instrument with rural origins into one that is highly regarded and central to Klasik Türk Müziği and TSM performance. Not only have Tanburi Cemil's playing style and melodic interpretations captivated listeners ever since, but the sound aesthetics of the instrument itself appealed to changing aesthetics in urban music compositions. Performer and music historian Fikret Karakaya wrote: "No doubt a significant factor in this was the fact that its sound was more compatible with the entirely more emotional and sad style that Turkish music had taken on in the beginning of the twentieth century" (2005, 26).

Tanburi Cemil's *klasik kemençe* recordings (CD track 20, "Eviç Taksim"), like his *tanbur* recordings, have come to define the modern style of *klasik kemençe* playing imitated by all contemporary performers. He also recorded a number of Aegean and Istanbul folk songs, a practice that continues to be followed by new generations of *kemençeci* as well. Thus, the *klasik kemençe* today, more than other art-music instruments, is used to perform both the urban art and the urban folk musics of Istanbul and Izmir. Contemporary groups like İncesaz (CD track 21), who perform contemporary arrangements of urban art and folk music, through their repertoire choices continue to blur the distinction between art music and other kinds of urban music.

> **ACTIVITY 2.3** *Become familiar with the solo sound of the two* kemençe-*s by listening to CD track 9* (Karadeniz) *and track 20* (klasik). *Then, listen to ensemble recordings and try to pick out the instrument (*Karadeniz kemençe: *tracks 4, 10, 23, 24;* klasik kemençe: *tracks 13, 21).*

2.10   CONCLUSION

Due to the forcefulness of the 1920s ban on Ottoman music forms and Mevlevi Sufism, and the decline in Ottoman-language education (few today learn to read in the Arabic script used for Ottoman Turkish), throughout much of the twentieth century Klasik Türk Müziği had limited popularity. Since the early 2000s, Klasik Türk Müziği has seen perhaps its greatest resurgence ever, as it has become popular with urban Muslim youth movements as a morally acceptable alternative to the risque lyrics and alcohol-serving performance contexts of pop music. Most notable, for the first known time significant numbers of pious Muslim women have taken to studying instruments like the oud, *tanbur*, and *ney*, and many have subsequently become recognized as among the best current musicians and teachers. One hundred years ago Greek and *Roman* female oudists recorded wax cylinders, setting a precedent for modern female oudists such as Gülçin Yahya Kaçar (b. 1966). However, for customarily "male" instruments such as the *ney* flute, the sudden emergence of female *neyzen* (*ney* master) Burcu Karadağ (b. 1979) as one of the most sought-after teachers was surprising to many in the older generation of art-music performers and fans.

Looking at Ottoman-era urban cultural life in retrospect, as a whole phenomenon as well as in considering the lives of individual composers and musicians, the lines between different social, religious, and ethnic backgrounds, the dichotomy of sacred versus secular music, and the connections between myriad genres of instrumental, vocal, and sacred musics were regularly blurred. Although the Ottoman Empire was in a state of decline during the dawn of audio-recording technology, many early recordings of Klasik Türk Müziği have survived. These recordings have recently come to have an unprecedented significance as the sole exemplars of proper performance practice on several instruments, and they continue to be scrutinized, analyzed, and mimicked today by younger generations of musicians.

In Istanbul today, Turkish-language TSM has supplanted most other art-music genres, but ethnicity questions continue in the complex, genre-crossing performances of *Roman* musicians. The performance of *fasıl*, in light of the sentimental lyrics and performers who cross conventional gendered boundaries, also raises significant questions about gender and sexuality in modern Turkey. Chapter 4 will consider in greater detail how *fasıl* (the repertoire, musical aesthetics, mode of performance, as well as some of the gender ambiguities) became the basis for most Turkish-language pop music. The next chapter will explore musical aspects of urban and rural musics, particularly the concept of *usul*, which was central to the teaching of *şarkı* in the *cemiyet* context.

CHAPTER 3

Musical Features: Time and Dramatic Tension

This chapter presents two musical concepts essential for understanding the vast majority of musical styles originating in Turkey. The first is musical time, in particular local concepts of meter and rhythm. *Usul* is a system of named rhythmic meters central to urban art music. Many individual *usul*-s in urban art music likely had origins in rural music, and thus the *usul* system is largely shared between the two. One particular family of asymmetrical *usul*-s that figures prominently in urban and rural music (and accounts for most of the examples on the listening CD) is *aksak*, which literally means "limping." The first and second sections will help you feel and understand basic *usul*-s. The third and fourth sections will help you hear how the same *usul* structure can be embellished to produce different rhythms, and these sections will help you understand the relation of *usul* to regional folk dances.

The second concept is the creation of dramatic tension. One way musicians create dramatic tension in Anatolian music is to structure performances as a dialogue between "question" (*soru*) and "answer" (*cevap*) phrases—the subject of Section 5. Another way to create tension is to perform melodies that follow defined melodic contours (*seyir*) but play with listeners' expectations of the arrival of the note that signifies the end of a melody (*durak*), the topic of Section 6.

3.1 USUL, BEAT STRUCTURES, AND METER

Usul is everywhere, yet you almost never hear it. It is part of what is performed in music, an abstraction of a work's rhythms, but not typically a rhythm performed by itself. When I took conservatory courses in *sanat* (urban art) music at Istanbul Technical University, the first stage for learning new compositions involved singing the song using Western solfege syllables while tapping the *usul* on my thighs with my palms, which is also how *usul* is taught at the *cemiyet*-s. When friends taught me to do regional, folkloric line dances, they first demonstrated how many main steps were in the dance and how the dance was counted. The pattern of steps nearly always matched the pattern of the *usul*. I remember many concerts where professional folk- and *arabesk*-music singers expressively waved with their left hand while singing, keeping *usul* like a conductor might keep time, although they were not cueing any musicians. But what is the *usul*, and why do you see it, feel it, dance it, but rarely hear it? And how does *usul* relate to rhythm?

An usul *is a named pattern of long and short beats that is tempo independent and defines the beat structure and meter of a piece of music.*

ACTIVITY 3.1 *In "Sabahtan Kalkan Kızlar" (CD track 4), a percussionist plays a repeating pattern of four strokes corresponding to the song's* usul *on a* bendir *(frame drum). There are numerous ways to embody the feeling of this* usul. *Listen first, clapping along with the* bendir. *If you are familiar with line dances, the basic step is a grapevine weave moving to the right: side step, step behind the support foot, side step, step across in front of the support foot. Try it.*

One characteristic of the *türkü* "Sabahtan Kalkan Kızlar" you may have noticed while "keeping *usul*" in Activity 3.1 is that the time between strokes differed, yet this pattern recurred throughout the song. You may have found yourself clapping slightly earlier or later than certain sounds on the recording. Like many examples from Turkey, this song features an asymmetrical **beat structure** and would be notated with an asymmetrical **meter**. The four beats of "Sabahtan Kalkan Kızlar" consist of two different durations: a short beat and a slightly longer one, creating a temporal asymmetry. This long-short-short-long beat pattern regularly recurs, and as the pattern has internal asymmetry, we say the piece has an asymmetrical beat structure.

Music with asymmetrical beat structures is tricky to notate, as Western notation was designed for music with a regular musical pulse (for example, the human heartbeat). Rural music was orally transmitted and not notated until the twentieth century. Starting during the folklore expeditions of the 1920s (Chapter 1), folklorists notated pieces using

Western meters, systematically subdividing short beats into two and long beats into three. This practice became standardized with Bartók's transcriptions of Adana-region folk music made in the late 1930s (Öztürk 2004, 168). Thus, "Sabahtan Kalkan Kızlar," which has a long-short-short-long pattern, is now notated in a $\frac{10}{8}$ time signature (3+2+2+3), an asymmetrical meter with ten pulses, but is *felt* as having four beats, which may or may not be accurately represented by the notation.

ACTIVITY 3.2 *Listen again to "Sabahtan Kalkan Kızlar" (CD track 4), counting aloud "long-short-short-long" in time with the* bendir. *When you are comfortable with that, focus on one instrument (*kemençe, guitar, cura*) to decide whether it always, sometimes, or rarely plays on the beat. Do that for the other two instruments, one at a time. Next, practice speaking/ counting a pattern of ten pulses, "ONE-two-three-FOUR-five-SIX-seven-EIGHT-nine-ten," placing emphasis on pulses one, four, six, and eight. Now listen again to track 4, counting in that manner. Which way makes it easier for you to follow the piece?*

It is important to distinguish between the notation of time, and the perception or feel of time, in Anatolian music. Musicians, dancers, and listeners would not perceive "Sabahtan Kalkan Kızlar" as having ten short, identical pulses but rather as having an *usul* consisting of a pattern of four beats. In many musical examples, if one subdivides short beats into two pulses and long beats into three pulses, one finds that the time between subdivisional pulses of short and long beats *is not the same*. As Western notation can only precisely indicate durations that have a simple integer relation to others (e.g., half, twice, or three times), the subtle nuances of *usul* and rhythm in Turkey cannot be precisely notated. This is where the difference between beat structure and meter becomes most significant. Emphasizing the beat structure of *usul* highlights the recurring pattern of short and long beats—how the music is felt. However, music in Turkey is often notated through a system that assumes a regular pulse and defines a musical meter. Notation for Anatolian music is often slightly off and needs to be interpreted with knowledge of how *usul* works in that locality, region, or musical genre.

3.2 ASYMMETRICAL BEAT STRUCTURES AND THE FEEL OF *AKSAK*

Most *usul*-s originate in regional folk-dance styles and are two, three, or four beats long. Asymmetrical *usul*-s originating in dance styles are known as *aksak*, which literally means "limping." The idea of "limping rhythms" is key to understanding Anatolian music and its relation to dance, as the asymmetry of the beat corresponds to the on-balance and off-balance steps and body movements of folk dances. When you feel the limp of *aksak*, it is easier to feel Anatolian music. This section introduces the most common *usul*-s that are *aksak*; the next section covers how musicians create rhythms within a particular *usul*.

Türk Aksağı The most basic *aksak*-type *usul*—called *Türk aksağı*—consists of two beats, one short and one long. In Figure 3.1, the feel and beat structure of *Türk aksağı* is indicated in the rectangular blocks (short-long). Above the blocks is a standard notation of *Türk aksağı* in $\frac{5}{8}$ time signature. Notes with up-stems indicate beats that are typically stronger (for *Türk aksağı*, the first beat), while notes with down-stems are typically weaker beats (the second beat). When "keeping *usul*" (using one's hands to mark the short and long beats), up-stems (strong beats) are marked with the left hand, and down-stems (weak beats) with the right. Below the blocks is an alternative notational system using the syllables *düm* and *tek*. Any rhythm that can be played on indigenous drums can be spoken using the syllables *düm* and *tek*, which come from Arab rhythmic modes (called *īqā'*). In all regions, *düm* (D) represents the lowest sound possible on a drum, while *tek* (T) is a contrasting higher-pitched sound (Marcus 2007, 60). Dots between *düm* and *tek* syllables indicate rests, or moments without a strong accent.

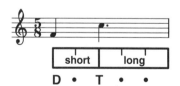

FIGURE 3.1   Türk aksağı usulu. *Tick marks in the rectangular blocks indicate subdivisional pulses; thus, the short beat can be subdivided into two pulses, and the long beat into three.*

Türk aksağı can also be reversed, with the long beat first (Figure 3.2):

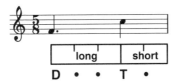

FIGURE 3.2   Türk aksağı usulu *variant*.

ACTIVITY 3.3 *Listen to two examples of* Türk aksağı *(CD tracks 5, 9, 22) while keeping* usul *with the palms of your hands. You can either slap your thighs or a tabletop, maintaining a left-hand, right-hand pattern corresponding with the strong and weak beats. While keeping* usul, *determine if the two are short-long or long-short examples. What events in the music made you choose one or the other? Be ready to articulate the reasons. Note: "Zamanı Gelir" (track 5) has musical accents that are not in the* usul—*be careful to only mark two moments per musical measure with your hands.*

Devr-i Turan **and** *Devr-i Hindi.*   Two different *aksak*-type *usul*-s have one long and two short beats and are notated using a $\frac{7}{8}$ time signature. *Devr-i turan usulu* is ordered long-short-short (Figure 3.3), while *devr-i hindi usulu* (sometimes called *mandıra*) is ordered short-short-long (Figure 3.4).

ACTIVITY 3.4 *The listening CD has two examples of* devr-i hindi *(CD tracks 23, 24; see also Figure 4.3) and one of* devr-i turan *(CD track 7). Listen to these while keeping* usul *(left-right-right, in that order, for all examples in both* usul*). Be careful not to equate the left-right-right hand patterns with long and short beats.*

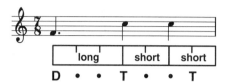

FIGURE 3.3 Devr-i turan usulu.

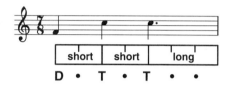

FIGURE 3.4 Devr-i hindi (mandıra) usulu.

These two beat structures underlie two very different dance forms. The short-short-long *usul* underlies many local varieties of *horon* line dances from the Eastern Black Sea (Figure 1.11). In contrast, the long-short-short *usul* often is found in the *semah* sacred dance done by the Alevis (Figure 1.2). Two different *usul*-s, two different dances, two very different kinds of music.

If you have had no trouble feeling the *usul* so far and understand notated time signatures, you may be interested to learn that some *horon* dance pieces notated in $\frac{7}{8}$ are actually not in the *devr-i hindi usulu*. These songs are played so fast (search on YouTube for Kazım Koyuncu's live performance of "Tabancamın Sapını") that the first two short beats blend together into a single, longer pulse. *Horon* dances at this speed have two steps, not three, and thus two musical beats in the *usul*, the first slightly longer than the second. When notated, the long beat would have four subdivisions, while the short would have three. Therefore, a $\frac{7}{8}$ time signature does not immediately indicate whether a piece has two or three beats per measure, how the measure might be subdivided, and whether subdivided beats have a consistent pulse. One has to know additional details about the piece—its region of origin and the specific dance it accompanies (if a dance-music piece)—in order to determine the *usul* and the proper feeling.

Four–Beat *usul*-s. Numerous *aksak*-type *usul*-s feature four-beat patterns. You already learned about one such *usul* when listening to "Sabahtan Kalkan Kızlar." This is an example of *aksak semai* (also known as *curcuna*) and the long-short-short-long pattern (Figure 3.5).

FIGURE 3.5   Aksak semai (*or* curcuna) usulu.

ACTIVITY 3.5   *Two strikingly different musical forms use* aksak semai: türkü *(Chapter 1) and* saz semaisi *(Chapter 2). The duration of one cycle of long-short-short-long in the* türkü *(CD track 4, 28) is about two and a half seconds, versus five to six seconds for the* saz semaisi *(CD track 15, 17). Listen to the four examples while keeping* usul *(left-right-left-right). In which examples is the* usul *more prominently heard?*

Perhaps the most commonly used *usul* of the *aksak* type is, appropriately, simply called *aksak*. It features one long beat and three short beats, either in the short-short-short-long pattern (Figure 3.6) or the long-short-short-short pattern (Figure 3.7).

The short-short-short-long version is the basis of the *karşılama* couples dance and most *Roman oyun havası* (Chapter 2), and also is a common *usul* for TSM *şarkı*-s such as "Mahrum-i Şevkim" (see Section 5 for an analysis of this piece). A variant of this *usul* performed in a very slow fashion, *ağır aksak usulu,* is the basis of the *zeybek* dance (Chapter 1).

ACTIVITY 3.6   *Compare* aksak *in a* Roman oyun havası *(CD track 18, Figure 3.11), in the Eastern Black Sea* türkü *"Sümela" (CD track 10), in the TSM* şarkı *"Mahrum-i Şevkim" (CD track 12, Figure 3.13), and in a* zeybek *dance (CD track 2, Figure 3.12). While listening, keep* usul, *left-right-left-right. Decide which example you think most emphasizes the* usul, *and which emphasizes it the least. Articulate the musical reasons for your decision; for example, the presence or absence of strong accents, or the ways individual instruments either emphasize or avoid the* usul.

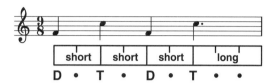

FIGURE 3.6   Aksak usulu.

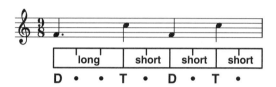

FIGURE 3.7   Aksak usulu *variant*.

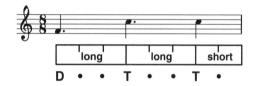

FIGURE 3.8   Nim sofyan usulu.

Nim Sofyan.   While most dances relating to the preceding *aksak usul*-s feature primary steps that correspond with the *usul* and render physical the asymmetry, that is not the case with *nim sofyan*. A commonly found *usul* with a three-beat structure, *nim sofyan* consists of two long beats and one short beat (Figure 3.8, CD track 25). Although this is asymmetrical like the preceding examples, it is not *aksak* (limping), as the *halay* and *misket* dances (Chapter 1) using *nim sofyan* have two even-length steps per measure, rather than emphasizing the *usul*'s three asymmetrical beats.

Combination *Usul*-s.   Most musics in Turkey are based on two-, three-, or four-beat *usul*-s. However, some Ottoman art-music compositions, and slower and more esoteric rural songs (particularly heavy epic poetic forms such as *destan türküsü* and Alevi *deyiş*) use longer beat structures that combine two or more *usul*-s shown above. For example,

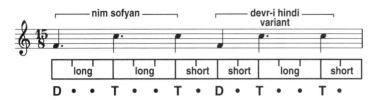

FIGURE 3.9 Raksan usulu *(from the* deyiş *"Ey Zahit Şaraba Eyle İhtiram").*

the *deyiş* "Ey Zahit Şaraba" by Edip Harabi (CD track 8) features *raksan usulu* (Figure 3.9) during the vocal melody from 0:26.

When notated, *raksan usulu* has a $\frac{15}{8}$ time signature, which in practice is felt as a measure of *nim sofyan* (long-long-short) followed by a measure of a variant of *devr-i hindi* (short-long-short). When thought of as long-short patterns, the correct feel is maintained, and musicians (and listeners) do not need to count to fifteen.

ACTIVITY 3.7 *Listen to the* deyiş *"Ey Zahit Şaraba Eyle İhtiram" (CD track 8). Make a timing chart that indicates when vocal and instrumental sections occur (in minutes: seconds). The timing chart will help you easily find the vocal and instrumental sections in the song. Put this timing chart next to Figure 3.9, and listen back to the vocal sections while keeping* usul *(left-right-right-left-right-right). The first syllable of the vocal line corresponds to the first beat of* raksan usulu, *and raksan only happens during the vocal sections. How many measures of* raksan *are in each vocal section? Notate this on your timing chart. Finally, listen just to the two instrumental breaks (between vocal phrases) to determine their* usul *(hint: each break uses an asymmetrical beat structure that you learned about earlier, and both are in a different* usul).

So far I have presented what I believe to be the simplest system for understanding the variety of asymmetrical beat structures found in Anatolian music. Musicologist and *saz* performer Okan Murat Öztürk, in his monograph about *zeybek* musical culture, notes that there is a tension between competing theories of *usul*. Some theorists treat *usul*-s simply as meters (e.g., $\frac{9}{8}$), others as particular rhythmic patterns (corresponding to the most common percussion rhythm that might be played to accompany a piece within a particular meter), and others yet as beat patterns (2006, 167–71).

Although many rhythmic concepts are shared between Turkish *usul* and neighboring rhythmic systems, there is a key difference between Turkish *usul* and Arab *īqā'*: *usul* is tempo and timbre independent, while *īqā'* is tempo and timbre dependent. In Turkey, the three-beat *usul* named *nim sofyan* (long-long-short) might be *spoken* as D••T••T• but in practice could be *performed* as D••T••D• or D••D••T•—all three are still *nim sofyan*. In the *īqā'* system, this rhythmic mode has different names when performed slower (*waḥda*) or faster (*malfūf*), or when the timbre pattern varies (D••D••T• is different than D••T••T•). Turkish *usul* is less specific and more flexible regarding timbre; because of this, I do not emphasize the *düm-tek* system for describing *usul*, as the ideal use for these syllables in Anatolian music is in describing specific performed drum rhythms.

3.3   RHYTHMS MADE WITHIN *AKSAK* BEAT STRUCTURES

The analysis so far has been on the *usul*-s that structure much Anatolian music (particularly, *aksak* beat structures), but not on the rhythms that can be played within a specific *usul*. There are four key points about the relation between *usul* and rhythm:

The *usul* is rarely played in isolation as a discrete musical part.

In ensemble performances, each performer embellishes the *usul* in a different way, resulting in a layering of simultaneously occurring different rhythms.

Choices about how to embellish an *usul* may be specific to an individual piece, or to the performance practice of a specific locality or genre.

The feel of a rhythm and the likelihood that the *usul* will be prominently emphasized are dependent on the tempo at which a piece of music is performed.

Embellishment refers to adding events between the beats and possibly leaving out events directly on the beats of an *usul*, resulting in a unique rhythm. Regarding points one and two, the *usul requires* embellishment. One striking characteristic of Anatolian ensemble performance is that, even when the whole ensemble plays the same melody, the rhythm of the melody each musician plays is slightly different. When a singer and instrumentalist perform simultaneously, the instrumentalist may add rhythmic embellishments that the singer does not sing. On top of that, percussion embellishments tend to be quite different than melodic embellishments, and multiple percussion instruments typically embellish differently from each other (see Activities 3.8, 3.9). These different rhythmic layers in combination result in a **heterorhythmic** texture. In Anatolian ensemble performance, each rhythmic layer relates to the *usul,* but no part by itself is identical to the *usul* nor considered to be "the rhythm" of the piece.

So how does a performer know what rhythm to play, and what defines an appropriate way to embellish an *usul*? Ideas about appropriate rhythms are specific to individual songs or localities, and this knowledge continues to be orally transmitted between musicians. For example, a *davulcu* (*askı-davul* player) does not learn how to "play *Türk aksağı*"—he or she learns how to create appropriate rhythmic embellishments for *specific songs* based on the *Türk aksağı usulu* (Figures 3.10, 4.8). A *saz* player does not learn a single picking style for use in all *devr-i turan* pieces but instead learns techniques and conventions for performing the music of a specific locality or region in an appropriate manner.

The *usul* system is tempo independent, but tempo and musical function are critical for determining the appropriateness of specific rhythmic embellishments. For example, two dance types, the *karşılama* and *zeybek,* both use the four-beat *aksak usulu.* The *karşılama* is a fast-paced couples dance with four steps where partners move symmetrically while facing each other. In many *karşılama* performances, the song melody and the percussive embellishments, like the dance steps, consistently emphasize the *usul's* four beats. The *zeybek* dance, on the other hand, is less than one-quarter the speed of the *karşılama* and has no similarity in feel despite also being in *aksak usulu.* It is much harder to "find the beat" in *zeybek* performances, as many drum or melodic-instrument embellishments create **syncopations**—accents that do not fall on the *usul's* beats—and the dance is often syncopated in relation to both the *usul and* the melodic and percussive accents. Likewise, in art music, *curcuna* and *aksak semai* technically describe identical long-short-short-long *usul-s,* but works in *curcuna* are much faster and more likely in practice to feature a strongly articulated beat, while works in *aksak semai* are slow and often feature extensive syncopation.

To illustrate these points, I will show how four distinct musical parts embellish the *Türk aksağı usulu* in a recording of the Lazuri-language folk song "Lazepeşi Duğuni," sung by Fatih Yaşar. The rhythm section of this contemporary arranged recording includes both a Western drum set and a *djembe* (West African goblet drum), each of which embellishes the *usul* in a different way (Activity 3.8).

ACTIVITY 3.8   *Listen to "Lazepeşi Duğuni" (CD track 22, 0:10) while reading along with Figure 3.10. First, note how the kick drum pattern (on the "drums" staff) aligns with the basic two-beat* Türk aksağı *(on the "usul" staff). Then, note how snare drum accents are syncopated (do not align with the* usul*). Third, note how the high hat usually articulates a steady eighth-note pulse. Fourth, listen for the* djembe *hand drum, whose accents do not usually fall on the beat. Then, listen to the vocal and the* tulum *bagpipe renditions of the song melody, each of which features a different stress pattern. While the* tulum *accents the fifth eighth-note of most measures, there is no event on that beat subdivision for most of the chorus vocals.*

No one part performs the *usul* literally (the kick drum comes the closest, matching the *usul* on measures 1, 2, 3, 5, 6, and 7), and every subdivision is accented at some point during the eight-bar chorus melody. Yet, the piece is unquestionably "in *Türk aksağı*."

Another performance of "Lazepeşi Duğuni" would probably share many rhythmic characteristics with this one. If the instrumentation were *askı-davul, kemençe,* and voice, the *davulcu* would likely play something rhythmically related to what the drummer performed for this track, the *kemençeci* would probably play something similar to the *tulum* part, and the singing would feature similar stress patterns. Why is this?

Knowledge of how to rhythmically articulate this particular piece is passed down orally from musician to musician and, more recently, through commercial and shared field recordings. Some of this knowledge is less specific to this particular piece but pertains to

FIGURE 3.10 *Rhythmic embellishments in "Lazepeşi Duğuni." In the drums part, the high hat is notated with "x" note heads, and the kick drum and snare drum are the lower and higher regular note heads. The* usul *part is not performed, but shown for reference.*

the performance of *horon* dance pieces in the town of Ardeşen (in the Rize Province of the Eastern Black Sea). A melody similar to "Lazepeşi Duğuni" from Rize (to the west) or Hopa (to the east) would likely be embellished differently due to local differences in performance practice. Professional musicians today know not only the rhythmic embellishment styles specific to one or two towns but those of many localities and regions across Turkey. Media technologies—television and radio broadcasts, commercial recordings, and media-rich websites—have been integral to the development and spread of this nationally held knowledge of local practices. Yet, the use of media technologies has not led to a homogenization of playing styles but rather to a multiplicity of styles that manifests as a national consciousness about local and regional cultural differences.

3.4 COMPARISON OF RHYTHMIC LAYERS IN *KARŞILAMA* AND *ZEYBEK* DANCE FORMS

To reiterate, *usul* is tempo independent and elaborated in dramatically different ways depending on the tempo. Of the many different ways of performing *aksak usulu*, no two differ more than those found in the Thracian *karşılama* and Aegean *zeybek* dances. Thracian *karşılama*-s range in tempo from roughly ♪=180 to ♪=300, and melodic and percussion rhythms often feature a fairly constant eighth-note pulse. Figure 3.11 shows the main eight-bar melody to "Kiremit Bacaları" (CD track 18, Activity 3.9), a *Roman karşılama* from Keşan, a town west of Istanbul. *Zeybek* dances, like those done to the song "Karyolamın Demiri" (CD track 2, Figure 3.12), are extremely slow, with a notated pulse of ♩=50 (slower than the human heartbeat at rest). Just one measure of

FIGURE 3.11   *Elaboration of* aksak usulu *in "Kiremit Bacaları."*

"Karyolamın Demiri" is nearly twice as long as the entire eight-measure melody of "Kiremit Bacaları."

ACTIVITY 3.9   *Heterorhythmic texture in "Kiremit Bacaları" (CD track 18). Listen through several times. First, become comfortable finding the* usul. *This may be more difficult than in preceding examples, as all of the musical parts have strong syncopation, and like many other* Roman oyun havası *used for* karşılama *dance, the melody begins on the* usul's *second beat. I have given you two track timings in Figure 3.11 (0:10 and 0:24) to help. Then, with a friend, listen through the piece while one of you keeps the* usul *and the other taps the* davul *rhythm. Note how the occasional sixteenth notes in the* davul *pull you towards the next downbeat and also add rhythmic tension. Third, listen individually for each melody instrument. Tap or speak the clarinet melody (ignoring the pitches) as though it were a percussion instrument, in order to find the "clarinet rhythm." Have your friend do the same for the* kanun *rhythm. Pay attention for moments in measures 3–5 when the* kanun *rhythm differs from the clarinet rhythm.*

Unlike the consistent density of the *karşılama, zeybek* performances feature frequent contrasts in rhythmic density, switching from thirty-second-note melodic passages to long held notes. The dance, too, features strong contrasts between still poses, where the dancer has his arms straight out to the sides and is balanced on only one leg, and rapid motion, perhaps a lunge followed by several subtle quick steps (see the book's website for video examples). Figure 3.12 is a transcription of one specific *zeybek*, "Karyolamın Demiri" (CD track 2). The *davul* rhythm is fixed and precomposed, and specific to this piece. There is no generic "zeybek rhythm," and other *zeybek*-s from the Aegean may have similar or considerably different embellishment patterns. However, most *zeybek*-s have a similar dramatic tension, created largely through contrasting rhythms (see Activity 3.10).

FIGURE 3.12 *Elaborations of* ağır aksak usulu *in "Karyolamın Demiri."*

ACTIVITY 3.10 *Go through Figure 3.12 with a ruler aligned vertically to track when two or more parts perform together. You can see that this* zeybek *consists of multiple independent rhythmic streams that only vaguely appear to relate. However, the parts all coincide on the* usul's *last short beat. Is there any other moment when all the parts simultaneously articulate a sound?*

3.5 MUSICAL FORM: *SORU-CEVAP*

Most composed music and folk songs featuring instruments and voice is based on a "question-answer" form called *soru-cevap*. Unlike call-and-response forms, typically each *cevap* (answer) phrase is unique and rarely is a repeat of the *soru* (question). Sometimes there is a clean break between the question and the answer, but often the two overlap by one or more notes. Rather than thinking of a song as consisting of a single continuous melody, it is often helpful to think of songs as consisting of two melodic streams, which may or may not overlap for brief moments.

One of the first things to notice about *soru* and *cevap* phrases is that they are orchestrated very differently. The aesthetic goal (regardless of ensemble size) is to make the sound of the *cevap* as distinct as possible from the sound of the *soru*. In performances when a solo singer accompanies herself or himself on *saz* or *kemençe*, this effect is achieved through changing volume, ornamentation, playing style, and/or note density. Answers are often louder, with more variety and complexity of ornaments and a higher density of notes than the instrumentation for question phrases. In large-ensemble arrangements, the majority of the orchestra refrains from playing during vocal (question) phrases, and soloists do not sing during answers. Thus, there is a palpable change in ensemble texture between *soru* and *cevap* phrases.

Another feature of answer phrases is that they often lead into the singer's next question phrase by ending on or suggesting the note where the singer will begin. C*evap* phrases help lead the singer—and the listeners—through the song. Few musics in Anatolia, for example, feature frequent, sudden leaps in register. *Cevap* phrases fill in the spaces, helping a question phrase ending at a low register to smoothly transition to a new question beginning at a high register. This structure is very characteristic of TSM *şarkı*-s such as "Mahrum-i Şevkim" by Rahmi Bey (CD track 12). In Figure 3.13, the passages underlined with square brackets are the *cevap* phrases, performed in the recording by the whole ensemble minus the chorus of singers.

ACTIVITY 3.11 *You have already heard several pieces with* soru-cevap *structures, including "Ey Zahit Şaraba" (CD track 8), "Âşık Oldur" (CD track 7), and "Bir Bahar Akşamı" (CD track 16). Four other notable examples are tracks 5, 12, 19, and 25. Listen to all seven of these again, focusing on the different orchestration of the two melodic streams—the* soru *and the* cevap. *How many alternations between question and answer happen in each? How long are the* cevap-s *in different styles of music? (Hint: there is considerable variance between some examples.) Choose two pieces and make a timing chart for each, noting the track timings when each question and answer begins.*

Regardless of the ensemble size or the musical genre, *cevap* phrases are one of the most creative moments in contemporary performances

FIGURE 3.13 Soru-cevap *phrases in "Mahrum-i Şevkim"* (cevap *shown in square brackets*).

of traditional and art-music repertoires. While vocal question phrases are usually through-composed and have little room for variability, *cevap* can be altered or even totally redesigned. Musical groups with a strong mutual understanding can collectively and spontaneously improvise new *cevap* during performances, which is exciting to audiences as it increases the dramatic tension of a performance of a previously known piece. This collective improvisational skill was something that impressed me when I conducted field research on the Istanbul State Turkish Music Ensemble in 1996, which you can hear in their recording of "Bir Gizli Günahın" (CD track 13). I subsequently found that this practice existed in *türkü* singing and Alevi performances as well. In Chapter 4 I will analyze the ornateness in *soru-cevap* orchestration of an arranged Alevi music recording.

3.6 MELODIC STRUCTURE: *SEYİR* AND *DURAK*

I introduced the concept of dramatic tension in relation to rhythmic contrasts (e.g., the *zeybek*) and unexpected *soru-cevap* phrases. However, dramatic tension in Anatolian music is most typically produced by the use of specific *seyir*-s—melodic contours—and a general tendency to prolong the ultimate arrival on the last note of a melody—the *durak*. *Seyir* and *durak* are two of the many aspects that define specific melodic modes (*makam*). A full treatment of the topic of *makam* is impossible in a book of this scope, as the *makam* systems of Klasik Türk Muziği, urban folk musics, and myriad rural traditions differ considerably, and certain aspects such as intonation are very complex (and the subject of considerable disagreement among scholars). The interested reader is encouraged to explore *makam* further through readings in the bibliography, particularly Karl Signell's book on *makam* in urban art music (1977) and Scott Marcus's *Music in Egypt* (2007).

Seyir and *durak* are two aspects of *makam* that are easy to hear and important for learning to hear the affect of melodies. The two are related, as the last note of any improvisation or song determines the pitch of the *durak* (*durak* means "resting place"), and the *seyir* can be conceived as the map of how the performers and listener travel to reach that inevitable point. The *durak* is octave-specific; the same pitch an octave up is not considered to be the *durak*. Although in some pieces the *durak* pitch recurs frequently throughout the melody, in other pieces the listener's first encounter with the *durak* happens at the very end of the piece of music. Listening for the *durak* is similar to listening to Turkish-language sentences, as typically the last word of a sentence is the verb, and the verb itself receives agglutinative suffixes identifying the subject, time, and case. Thus, the ends of phrases, musical or grammatical, are some of the most important moments that one listens for.

ACTIVITY 3.12 *Return to "Mahrum-i Şevkim" (Figure 3.13, CD track 12). Even if you don't read notation, you can look at the very last note of the score: the* durak *is the pitch A in the lower octave. Look through the rest of the score to see how often this pitch recurs (circle this on a photocopy of the score). Does the piece begin on the* durak? *If not, how much time passes before the* durak *is first heard? Do the same exercise with "Akşam Oldu Yine Bastı" (Figure 3.15, CD track 19). The* durak *is the half note right below the number two in the last measure.*

Seyir ranges from a general description of melodic contour (ascending, descending, or mixed ascending-descending) to a very specific road map detailing a sequence of important pitches that must occur before resting at the *durak*. A *seyir* is specific to a particular *makam*. Two pieces you heard already, "Mahrum-i Şevkim" (Figure 3.13, CD track 12, in *makam kürdîlihicazkâr*) and the *uzun hava* "Kalktı Göç Eyledi" (CD track 1, in *makam muhayyer*), are striking examples of descending-type *makam*-s, meaning that the main song melody begins high in the vocal register and slowly descends to the *durak*. In the case of "Mahrum-i Şevkim," the descent is perceived as beginning at the first vocal utterance (0:25) and extending until the first held low A (1:17). It is not until halfway through the piece that the primary melodic descent is considered complete. The descending *seyir* of "Kalktı Göç Eyledi," which begins at 1:17 (the first vocal phrase) and extends until 2:14, is an even more dramatic example.

The descending *seyir* is so characteristic of Turkish-language folk songs, it drew Béla Bartók to rural Turkey to make a number of field recordings and transcriptions. Bartók was interested in comparing Hungarian and Turkish melodies for shared origins, as one linguistic theory of the time suggested that Hungarians and Turks had a shared ancestry. The shared-ancestry theory did not end up being accurate, and Bartók concluded that there was no common origin for Hungarian and Turkish music, but the result was a collection of ornately detailed transcriptions of folk-music practices that have been invaluable to ethnomusicologists and folklorists ever since.

However, some *makam*-s used in both urban and rural musics have a more complex, "roadmap–style" *seyir*. The *İstanbul türküsü* "Akşam Oldu

Yine Bastı Kareler" (CD track 19), in *makam segah-maye*, has two notable descents, and the song resides within a smaller melodic ambitus (range) than the descending-*seyir* examples previously mentioned. What distinguishes *makam segah-maye* from other *makam*-s is the sequence of important pitches (see Figure 3.14 for a score for the whole song, including instrumental sections, and Figure 3.15 for a reduction of the vocal melody): starting on F♯ in measure 5, moving to and resting on D in measure 10, a long scalar descent from the high A down to the *durak* pitch of B (passing through F♮ instead of F♯) in measures 13–14, another descent from the high A to a resting place of low A (measures 16–18), and a final

FIGURE 3.14 *"Akşam Oldu Yine Bastı Kareler," with* cevap *phrases indicated in square brackets. After the first ending in measure 10, the piece jumps back up and repeats from measure 5, continuing down the page via the second ending (measure 11).*

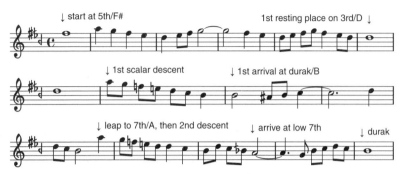

FIGURE 3.15 Seyir-durak *analysis of vocal-melody reduction for "Akşam Oldu Yine Bastı Kareler" (beginning at measure 5 of Figure 3.14).*

resolution to the final resting place—the *durak* itself (measure 20). Other *makam*-s may share the same pitches as *makam segah-maye*, but no other *makam* has this particular sequence of resting places.

> **ACTIVITY 3.13** *Listen to your two favorite examples on the CD with an ear towards melodic shape. Try drawing the ups and downs of the melody using a single continuous line (like a seismograph). Be ready to make a comparative statement about the shapes of the two pieces you drew in this manner.*

3.7 CONCLUSION

Through understanding the fundamentals of musical time (the feeling of *aksak*, and the distinction between *usul*-s and their embellished realizations in performance) and dramatic tension (created through rhythmic contrasts and the interplay between *soru* and *cevap* and between *seyir* and *durak*), you will be able to listen to most Anatolian music with a better sense of what makes the music work. In the following chapter, I will build on these elements and look at contemporary staged and performed arrangements of music based on urban and rural traditional music practices.

CHAPTER 4

Arranged Folk and Art Musics and New Musical Instruments

Ever since the first recordings were made in Turkey in the early 1900s (and perhaps much earlier), musical styles influenced by foreign popular musics of the time have thrived in urban Turkey. However, musicians in Turkey have rarely simply imitated foreign musical styles, but instead create fusions of Anatolian traditional and/or art musics with foreign musical elements. The process whereby traditional and art-music forms are adapted to new musical styles, in Turkey, is known as **arrangement**. Arrangements made in Turkey often feature many of the same instruments found in traditional music forms and use the same *makam* (melodic modes), *seyir* (melodic contours), and *usul* (beat structures). However, instead of creating solo or small-ensemble productions, arrangers in Turkey typically create complex, multipart, **polyrhythmic** arrangements equivalent in complexity to symphonic orchestrations of the European model.

Understanding arrangement is the key to understanding creativity in contemporary music making in Turkey, since the artful and tasteful performance or recording of a traditional music work is considered by many to have a greater value than the composition of something entirely new (Markoff 1990). To be an artful new performance or recording, an arrangement must preserve the local character (for *türkü* and *oyun havası*) or period-specific style (for Klasik Türk Müziği or TSM) of the original. Even Turkish rock bands cover *türkü* (Stokes 2002), and covers of previous generations of Anatolian rock classics (such as Erkin Koray's psychedelic rock pieces) are often more popular than newly composed songs. Arrangement is not just a part of the making of popular music but a practice that pervades the commercial music industry, the film and TV sector, and government folk- and art-music ensembles.

In this chapter I will focus on the arrangement of *türkü* and of various genres of art-music repertoires. This builds on the discussion of rural and urban music in the preceding chapters, turning attention to what happens when local and regional musical instruments are performed within a twenty-first-century digital-recording-studio context, and how the basic elements that structure Anatolian music (*usul, seyir, makam*) are part of popular, mass-marketed recordings and major concert performances. Outside the purview of this chapter are the many new songs written and performed by some of Turkey's rock and pop stars. That said, a considerable amount of today's top-selling popular music (including rock and pop) has its roots in Anatolian village practices or in urban *fasıl* singing.

Continuing the subject of the previous chapter, arrangements must preserve the primary accents of the *usul* of the original work. Whether the new arrangement has one *bendir* (frame drum) or over ten unique percussion instruments plus set drums, rhythmic embellishments must not be allowed to interfere with the basic *usul*. In a similar sense, singers and instrumentalists may freely embellish a melody and make it their own, but their ornaments must not overpower the original melody or alter the character of its *seyir* (melodic contour). Also, most arrangements not only preserve the *soru-cevap* form but often find creative ways to make questions and answers even more dramatic through innovative instrumentation.

One immediately apparent characteristic of many contemporary arrangements is the sheer diversity of musical instruments. Arrangers call for every instrument I have discussed so far, although not all instruments can be used in all arrangements. One of the themes in this book has been how music is part of the national consciousness about local and regional cultural differences. Arrangement, rather than breaking down these differences, has instead amplified them. In arranged recordings, certain instruments are so charged with meaning that they come to symbolize a locality or region itself.

In this chapter, I will present the concept of arrangement in several different musical contexts. In each, I will focus on different musical-cultural aspects. I hope that in doing so I can present a broad sonic picture of what is entailed in arrangement in Turkey and some sense of how local, regional, and historical music traditions are simultaneously changed and preserved through the creation of new recordings and staged performances. The first context is concert arrangement of urban art music in the performances of government art-music ensembles. I will discuss a 1990s concert by the Istanbul State Turkish Music

Ensemble, at the time the foremost art-music ensemble, and then a more recent recording by the group İncesaz, whose members have participated in similar government ensembles. The second context is the recently created, immensely popular genre known as "Karadeniz." I will compare two arrangements of the *horon* (Chapter 1) dance song "Bu Dünya Bir Pencere," one inspired by acoustic ensemble music and film scores, the other by indie rock. The third context is Alevi *deyiş türküsü*. I turn to a Dertli Divani recording that features a large, everchanging ensemble of different *saz*-family instruments. In the fourth context, I look broadly at *arabesk* popular music, particularly at ways in which *arabesk* arrangements preserve much of the urban *fasıl* aesthetic while evoking themes that are regionally significant to Southeastern and Eastern Anatolia. The fifth context explores one of the most important Kurdish pop-music tracks and how it draws on Kurdish traditional singing, *arabesk* arrangement, and *halay* dance motifs. The chapter concludes with a portrait of Erkan Oğur, a multi-instrumentalist and singer who has arranged many kinds of traditional music and invented "new" traditional music instruments that form an integral part of his arranged sound.

4.1 ARRANGEMENTS IN ART-MUSIC ENSEMBLES

As noted in Chapter 2, Klasik Türk Müziği was historically not an orchestral or large-ensemble genre but involved small groups. Typical Ottoman-era ensembles included the *ney-tanbur* duo, the oud-*kanun-violin* trio, and the *klasik kemençe-lavta* (a fretted instrument similar to the oud) duo, each of which performed distinct repertoires and repertoires that varied depending on the performance context. Art songs in both Osmanlıca and Turkish were, until the twentieth century, sung by a solo singer, and choral singing was not part of art-music practice.

During the formation of the Turkish Republic, Mustafa Kemal Atatürk and Mehmet Ziya Gökalp (who wrote many influential books on Turkishness and nationalism) believed that it was essential for the modern Turkish nation to have a modern Turkish music, yet one that still expressed the essential character of the Turkish people. They found in composer and ethnomusicologist Ahmed Adnan Saygun a kindred spirit. Ahmed Adnan, like Mehmet Ziya, found the contemporary performance of urban *fasıl* music to be distasteful and disorganized. They were responding to the ways in which musicians within a *fasıl* ensemble seemed to all perform their own interpretations of the song melody with apparent disregard for each other (CD track 9), resulting in a heterophonic texture. (This was characteristic primarily of *fasıl*, less so of other Anatolian genres).

Ahmed Adnan, who loved Turkish folk songs as well as Western orchestral music, wanted to create a polyphonic music performed by a symphony orchestra that drew on Turkish folk songs but dispensed with the heterophony of *fasıl*. Similar projects had been successful in Russia and Czechoslovakia, and most of all in Hungary (where his ethnomusicology teacher Béla Bartók had composed piano sonatas, string quartets, and symphonies based on Hungarian folk songs). However, Ahmed Adnan's compositions and his style of arranging did not catch on in Turkey. First, Western symphonic instruments were not capable of evoking the spirit of Anatolian folk instruments. Second, *fasıl* songs (TSM) were popular in Istanbul, and audiences were uninterested in hearing entirely new compositions in a radically new style. It became apparent that for a new national music to emerge, a greater connection to the roots of both urban art music and rural folk music needed to be maintained.

Mesut Cemil (1902–1963), the son of Tanburi Cemil Bey (whose recordings are important today in teaching and learning Ottoman art music), attempted a different approach, founding the first chorus dedicated to the singing of TSM songs. As TSM performance tended to involve an expressive and personalized singing style, it took considerable effort to create a style that worked as a choral music. Singers in his chorus learned to coordinate ornaments and to listen to each other closely in order to produce a unified, homogeneous sound aesthetic. What choral singers individually sang related to what they might sing in a solo concert, except that the *way* they interacted with each other was new. The choral singing style of CD tracks 12 and 13 is directly influenced by Mesut Cemil's chorus, the Istanbul Radio Turkish Classical Music Chorus, which was important not only in establishing an arranged musical style

but also in teaching and disseminating the modern Turkish language through radio broadcasts.

A similar change happened in instrumental art-music ensembles. New large ensembles were formed at government radio stations in Istanbul and Ankara. The orchestra director (a new artistic profession) carefully managed daily ensemble rehearsals. Some directors conducted with a baton, like Western orchestral conductors (Nevzat Atlığ, CD track 12). Others conducted while playing in the ensemble, and musicians developed an invisible cueing system and memorized the arrangement decisions made during rehearsals. Musicians in art-music ensembles today read single-line scores that are basically identical to those that would have been used in the nineteenth century, even by *fasıl* musicians. The difference between then and now is in arrangement—how a score is read, which instruments are selected to play, and how different parts combine to make an ensemble sound.

The Istanbul State Turkish Music Ensemble (İstanbul Devlet Türk Müziği Topluluğu) was formed in 1987 by Necdet Yaşar, who had first experienced large-ensemble performance of art music in the 1950s with Mesut Cemil and the Classical Music Chorus. When I observed the ensemble in 1996, in the last concert season that Necdet Yaşar directed before retiring, it consisted of the following performers:

2 *tanbur*

2 ouds

2 *klasik kemençe*

1 cello

1 *kanun*

2 *ney*

1 percussion—*daire, bendir, daf,* or *kudüm*

8–16 choristers—half men, half women

For some concerts, the ensemble enlisted a guest violinist or clarinetist, meaning that between eighteen and twenty-eight musicians performed at once.

ACTIVITY 4.1 *Listen to the Istanbul State Turkish Music Ensemble performance (CD track 13). Compare this with solo performances of Tanburi Cemil Bey (CD track 20) and Yorgo Bacanos (CD track 14), and the small-ensemble performance by Hafız Sadettin Kaynak (CD track 19), where no more than four musicians performed simultaneously. First, try to describe the similarities and differences in color or timbre between the four examples. Then listen carefully to the state-ensemble performance and try to hear individual instruments, particularly the oud and klasik kemençe.*

Figure 4.1 is a reproduction of the actual score used by the ensemble when performing the TSM *şarkı* "Bir Gizli Günahın" (CD track 13). The first thing to notice is that the score is part of the TRT (Turkish Radio and Television) repertoire. TRT, a division of the Turkish Culture Ministry, has created official scores for tens of thousands of works of Ottoman- and Turkish-language art and folk music. The second point is that many more notes are performed than what you see on the score. The notational style of TRT scores is known as **prescriptive notation**, meaning that it provides minimalist instructions to the performer on how to sound out the music. TRT scores depict the melodic contour of a piece and some of the more basic rhythmic features. However, considerable ornamentation is necessary to correctly perform the piece. For example, notated in measure 5 is a sixteenth-eighth-sixteenth-note figure. In the recording (0:28), the performers all play complex rhythmic figures instead of what is notated, as the figure for them is a shorthand for a set of possibilities for embellishing the melody. Some ornaments are intuitively performed by musicians without rehearsal, but others, such as the embellishment for measure 4 (0:28), involved debate. During many *cevap* phrases (0:37, 0:45, 1:08), you hear remnants of an older, prearranged *fasıl* performing style, as the oud and *kanun* play opposing fast scalar melodies that are not notated on the score.

A number of members of the Istanbul State Turkish Music Ensemble and other state art-music ensembles have formed small offshoot groups. One such group, İncesaz, premiers instrumental compositions and newly composed vocal *şarkı*-s by Cengiz Onural (b. 1961) and other contemporary TSM composers ("Tereddüt," CD track 21). The term *incesaz* historically referred to a small ensemble featuring stringed instruments and percussion. The most prominent melody instruments in İncesaz (and in historical *incesaz* ensembles) are the *klasik kemençe* of Derya Türkan (b. 1973) and the *tanbur* of Murat Aydemir (b. 1971; both state musicians). While the preceding examples focused on how Klasik Türk Müziği (track 20) and TSM (track 21) were reinvented as large-ensemble musics, İncesaz is a project more about recapturing an imaginary past, of an Istanbul that was wholly European and cosmopolitan. İncesaz's arrangement style draws on Italian, French, and Greek light art and popular music and uses tango and other "Latin" rhythms (CD track 21 features Engin Gürkey's [b. 1967] Latin percussion accompaniment), in order to create a light, modern art-music sound. The Latin flavors and European motifs of the new *şarkı* "Tereddüt" are not part of the composition itself, as the same song could just as easily be performed by a state ensemble or even an instrumental soloist, in which case it would

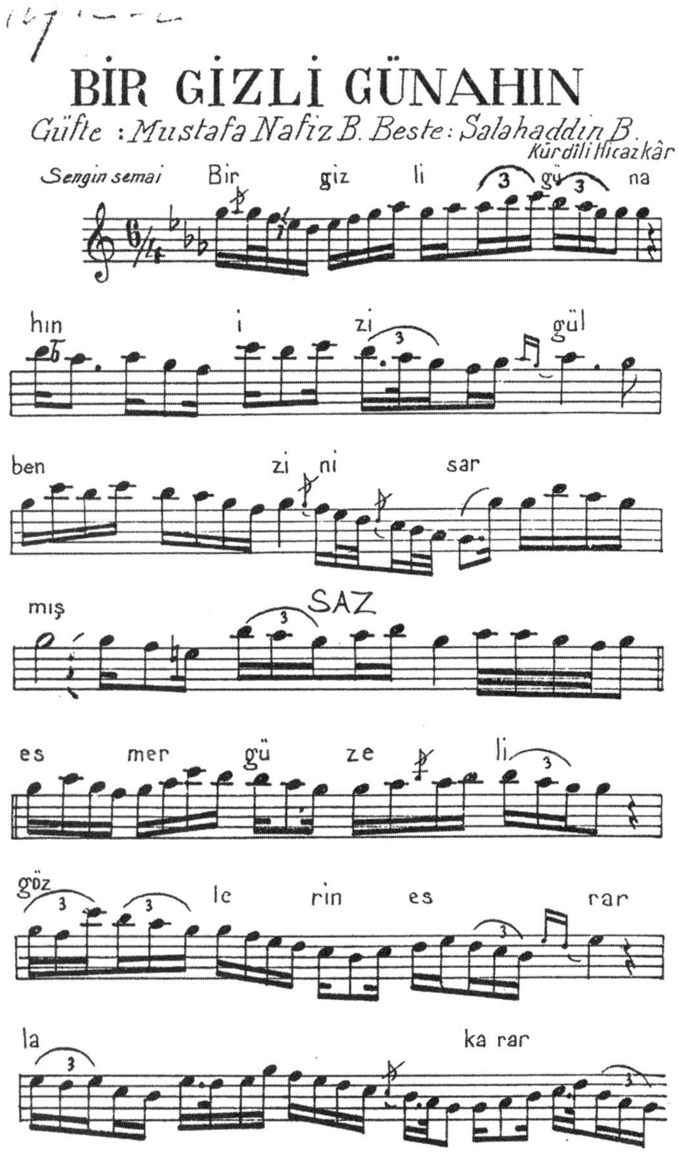

FIGURE 4.1 *Istanbul State Turkish Music Ensemble performance score for "Bir Gizli Günahın" composition (*beste*) by Selahattin Pınar, with lyrics (*güfte*) by Mustafa Nafiz Irmak. The text cut off at the top indicates the TRT repertoire number,* Sengin semai *is the* usul *of the piece, and* kürdîlihicazkâr *is the name of the* makam.

sound similar to other TSM *şarkı*. İncesaz also performs older *şarkı*-s and anonymously authored *türkü*-s, and all their recordings to an extent feature the eclectic arrangement style heard in "Tereddüt."

4.2 MAKING KARADENIZ MUSIC: "BU DÜNYA BİR PENCERE"

Certain arranging styles become so popular and imitated that they become known as new musical genres. A recent example, known by the regional name Karadeniz (tracks 4, 10, 22, 23, 24), consists of rural and urban folk songs from the Eastern Black Sea that are arranged for an ensemble consisting of a Western-style rock or jazz combo with Black Sea folk instruments performing the lead melodies. This is not the first time that many of these folk songs have been arranged. According to folklorist Arzu Öztürkmen, one of the most popular segments of Yurttan Sesler, a government radio program that broadcast ensemble arrangements of regional folk music to the nation starting in the 1940s, was Black Sea folk-dance music, particularly the fast *horon* dance pieces. Subsequent government orchestras also performed many of the same songs. From the 1980s, some *arabesk* and pop singers included Black Sea songs in their repertoire, but at the time it was not known as a "Karadeniz" genre distinct from other pop- and folk-music styles.

The late 1990s saw many commercially successful experiments with Karadeniz music. Kazım Koyuncu (1971–2005), an ethnically Laz singer from the town of Hopa near the Georgian border, pioneered a style known as "Laz rock," which following Kazım's death was continued by Laz rock groups such as Marsis (CD track 24). Fuat Saka (b. 1952) developed a jazz guitar style for playing Laz folk melodies (a similar style can be heard in Fatih Yaşar's recording of "Sabahtan Kalkan Kızlar," CD track 4). Singer Ayşenur Kolivar and the large pan-Anatolian performing ensemble Kardeş Türküler (Figure 4.2) created many arrangements of Hemşince-, Lazuri-, and Turkish-language folk songs for a large heterogeneous ensemble of Anatolian instruments (CD track 10). By 2005, when I began conducting my research on arranged folk music and Istanbul's recording studios, new artists in the nascent Karadeniz genre tended to view these three as significant influences, copying aspects of previous albums while making new ones. Striking to me at the time was how much of the musical content in arranged Karadeniz

FIGURE 4.2 *Kardeş Türküler performs pan-Anatolian arrangements of music sung in Turkish, Kurdish, Zazaki, Hemşince, Lazuri, Armenian, and other indigenous Anatolian languages.* (Courtesy of the Kalan Müzik Archive)

songs differed from field recordings, yet singers or instrumentalists sang or played song melodies nearly identically to traditional versions. In earlier publications, I wrote about how standardized audio-recording practices contributed to the creation of a Karadeniz genre (Bates 2010), and how part of the sound came from long-term, close interaction between a small number of arrangers and professional studio musicians (Bates 2008).

One way of understanding the effect of arrangement on traditional music practice is to compare arrangements of the same song. "Bu Dünya Bir Pencere" (This World Is a Window) is a classic *horon* dance song with a single melody and seven-syllable rhyming. The nine-measure melody (Figure 4.3) can be sung in nine seconds, with the verse and chorus sharing the identical melody. Even with three verses and three choruses, the song takes less than one minute to perform. So how do musicians create four- and five-minute arrangements of such a short song?

ACTIVITY 4.2 *Form a chorus with classmates. Be sure to include someone who can read Figure 4.3. Learn to sing the melody using any vocal syllables you wish.*

FIGURE 4.3   *Basic melody for "Bu Dünya Bir Pencere."*

One technique pioneered by the pan-Anatolian ethnic-fusion group Kardeş Türküler (see Chapter 5) involves making new sections out of very small fragments of the original melody. Arranger Aytekin Gazi Ataş (b. 1978; Figure 4.4), who performed with and arranged for Kardeş Türküler for several years, is particularly fond of this technique and often creates new *soru-cevap* passages out of a couple of notes of the original song melody.

Profile: Aytekin Gazi Ataş, a native of Tunceli-Dersim, began his professional music career in Kardeş Türküler, singing and playing *saz* and percussion on several albums and in concerts. Ethnically Zaza and Alevi, he has worked since 2004 as an arranger of numerous regional and popular genres of music and is best known for arranging the music to the TV series *Fırtına* (a Karadeniz-themed drama) and the feature films *Beynelmilel* and *Son Osmanlı.* His signature sound is a large ensemble of Anatolian folk instruments, notably *saz*-family instruments played in a "muted" style, a large backing percussion section, and subtle vocal sounds used as special effects.

Figure 4.5 diagrams the instrumentation of the intro to "Bu Dünya Bir Pencere" that Aytekin arranged for soloist Şevval Sam (CD track 23). Şevval Sam (b. 1973), a film actress and well-known TSM performer, began singing Karadeniz arranged folk music following a film role where she starred alongside Laz rock singer Kazım Koyuncu. What is depicted is the section at 1:44 that precedes the actual beginning of the first verse of the *türkü.* For the middle of the intro (diagram sections D and E), Aytekin invented a *soru-cevap* section, where the questions are performed on violin with *garmon* (a button accordion from Azerbaijan performed in a few Eastern Black Sea villages) and answered with plucked-string instruments. The question phrase is a variation of the song melody's sixth measure, but in the *soru-cevap* context it sounds entirely different. Aytekin uses this new phrase throughout the song, in passages between verses and choruses and in leading up to verses.

FIGURE 4.4   *Aytekin Gazi Ataş at work arranging sound for a TV series.*   *(Photo by Ladi Dell'aira)*

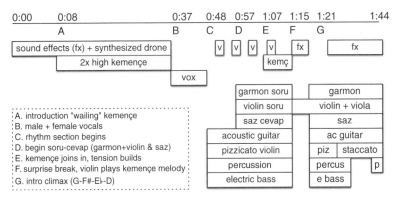

FIGURE 4.5   *"Bu Dünya Bir Pencere" introduction, arranged by Aytekin Ataş for Şevval Sam.*

It becomes a "second theme" in the piece. Aytekin also created entirely new melodic material, in particular the dramatic last section (G) with the slowly descending melody.

Şevval Sam's album was very well received and among the top-selling albums in Turkey in 2008. The Laz rock band Marsis included their own take of the same song on their 2009 debut album (CD track 24, Figure 4.6). Their introduction is shorter, only forty-two seconds, and, instead of featuring acoustic instruments and percussion, foregrounds rock guitars, electric bass, and drums. Marsis were influenced by the Şevval Sam recording and used the second theme that Aytekin had created as a *kemençe* melody in section B, although without the call and response. Marsis invented new melodic, harmonic, and rhythmic material for sections C and D.

The sound aesthetic of the two arrangements could not be more different. Aytekin's arrangement has a very "filmic" quality, enhanced by his use of drones, wind noise, and reverberant sound effects. Each of the eight sections in the introduction has a different ensemble sound, with between two and sixteen different instruments playing in any section. Marsis's version is aligned with indie-rock arrangements, using layers of different electric and acoustic guitars and contrasting drumset patterns. The staccato power chords at the end of section C break up the rhythmic groove that had been established. In contrast, Aytekin's arrangement features a more seamless rhythmic groove made of various hand percussion and pizzicato strings.

However, there are interesting commonalities. Both arrangements prominently feature *kemençe*, which grounds both as being Karadeniz as opposed to representing another region. Both feature acoustic guitars, an instrument ubiquitous in Karadeniz arrangements but not in the arrangements of other regional folk musics. When the songs actually begin, Korhan Özyıldız (Marsis's lead singer) and Şevval Sam sing a very similar song melody—five of the nine measures are identical. Also,

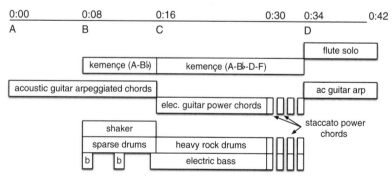

FIGURE 4.6   *"Bu Dünya Bir Pencere" introduction, arranged by Marsis.*

both arrangements feature a surprising break. For Aytekin's arrangement, the surprise is the solo violin interpretation of the second theme (section F); for Marsis, it is the *kaval* flute playing a brief improvisation with only guitar accompaniment (section D). Marsis' use of flute, in stark contrast to the preceding indie-rock style and power chords, suggests that Marsis, too, have been influenced by film-music soundscapes.

4.3 ALEVI ARRANGEMENTS: DERTLİ DİVANİ, "ZAMANI GELİR"

Dertli Divani is a prolific composer of new *deyiş türküsü* and one of the best-known living Alevi singers. As part of his musical path and activity as a *dede* (religious leader for Alevi ceremonies), Dertli Divani has done extensive field research in eastern Turkey, particularly in his hometown of Kısas (close to Şanlıurfa) and in the Maraş Province, collecting songs and knowledge about local performance practice. However, many of his recordings feature contemporary arrangements of traditional songs, *deyiş* composed by other living poets, and his own compositions. On his most recent album, *Hasbıhâl* (Kalan Müzik, 2005), he worked with several musician, arranger, and engineer teams at three studios. Unlike many Alevi artists, whose arrangements feature backing tracks consisting of a symphony of foreign instruments, Dertli Divani only employs Anatolian folk instruments, including dozens of different *saz*-family instruments, folk flutes, folk oboes, and *bendir*-s (frame drums). His arrangements often creatively play with the *soru-cevap* form discussed in Chapter 3.

In "Zamanı Gelir" (CD track 5), a *deyiş* composed by Âşık Mahrumi, the first 0:53 consists of an instrumental introduction that can be divided into two major question-answer phrases, with each answer phrase divisible into several shorter *soru-cevap* phrases. The questions and answers are distinguished by instrumentation (see Figure 4.7). The first *soru* (0:00–0:15) involves a melody played on a *bağlama* with a "muted" playing style, meaning that the notes are not allowed to sustain as they normally would, with rhythmic/chordal accompaniment on a short-necked *dedesaz* played with a fingernail *şelpe* technique. The first *cevap* (0:15–0:29) involves an embedded *soru-cevap* interchange between the *bağlama* (this time played with a pick and without the mute technique) and the *cura*. The second *soru* (0:29–0:37), although timbrally similar to the first one, has several different varieties of short-necked *dedesaz* played with fingernail *şelpe* style along with the muted *bağlama*. The second *cevap* (0:37–0:53)

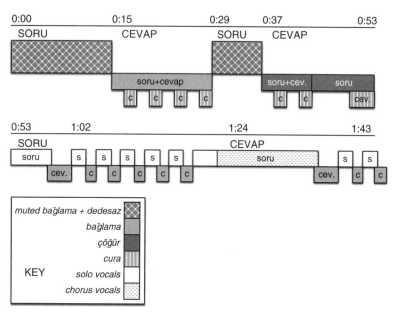

FIGURE 4.7   Soru-cevap *structure in "Zamanı Gelir."*

is similar to the first in instrumentation, except that the larger *çöğür* is used instead of *bağlama*. This introduction uses at least five unique *saz*-family instruments (Figure 4.8) and also showcases numerous *saz*-specific playing techniques. In a traditional performance of a *deyiş* like this, one or at most two *saz*-s would accompany the singing, and *soru-cevap* structures would be much simpler (an interchange between the singer and a single instrument). Dertli Divani uses the elements of traditional performance—regionally appropriate playing styles on indigenous instruments, the *soru-cevap* form, traditional *makam* (and *seyir*)—but creates a very modern work that is in no way "Westernized."

The recording of "Zamanı Gelir" was made by the engineer Hasan Karakılıç at Stüdyo Sistem, one of Istanbul's best-equipped digital recording studios. The process began with percussionist Ömer Avcı performing a basic *bendir* part on top of a metronomic click track. Then, two musicians performed all the *saz* parts. Hüseyin Albayrak and his cousin Ali Riza Albayrak are younger Alevi musicians who are experienced with arranging and working within the studio environment. On top of

FIGURE 4.8   Soru-cevap *structure in "Zamanı Gelir" (CD track 5).*

the *bendir* and click track, Ali Riza played a "plot" track on *bağlama* of the entire song melody, including the instrumental and vocal sections, but without distinguishing *soru* and *cevap* phrases. Then, Dertli Divani recorded a rough take of the vocals. The recording so far—one drum, one *saz*, one voice—was essentially a traditional, unarranged *deyiş*. This point is important, as good arrangements of Alevi music must have a firm basis in the traditional sound aesthetic.

With this basic version in place, the Albayraks brought dozens of *saz*-family instruments to the studio, including a very old *dedesaz*, several *cura*-s, *bağlama*-s, and *çöğür*-s made by Özbek Uçar and other makers, and other small three-stringed *saz*-s. I was not present during the creation of this song, but I observed the making of many similar arranged Alevi recordings and can speak generally about the process. Often, the first stage consists of rearranging the accompaniment in the vocal section. A new "rhythm *saz*" part was created to support Dertli Divani's singing and the instrumental intro, and a perfect "double" of that was immediately recorded. The two rhythm-*saz* parts were panned hard right and left. You can hear this in the first fifteen seconds of CD track 5 (the first line of Figure 4.8) and in the spaces between vocal sections. In a separate take, with a different *saz*, the *cevap* phrases echoing the vocal melodies were recorded, from start to finish, to separate tracks. Probably, the next step involved re-recording the melody of the instrumental intro with the muted technique on the *bağlama*. A different *bağlama* was used for the picked melody beginning at 0:15. Following that, a combination of strategic choices and a healthy amount of experimentation guided the subsequent recordings of perhaps over fifteen *saz*-family instruments. In the final arrangement, the largest ensemble is audible from 0:29–0:37.

It is likely this decision was made during the **editing** and **mixing** stages, and that an equivalent number of instruments had been recorded for other sections of the song. During editing, many sections of unique instrumental parts were probably deleted, as the musicians, Dertli Divani, or the engineer felt they did not work together. In normal arrangements, once the new parts are edited to satisfaction, the original *bağlama* plot track and the rough vocal track are removed, and final vocals are recorded on top of the arrangement. Mixing for this song was done within Cubase software, with the extensive use of EQ and reverb plugins. "Zamanı Gelir" uses techniques originally developed for Western pop- and rock-music productions in the 1960s (double tracking and EQ), the 1970s (extreme layering, reverb), and the 1990s (nonlinear digital-audio editing). However, in this context, they are used for the creative arrangement of a many-centuries-old tradition of sacred/secular music.

4.4   ARABESK

Since the late 1960s, *arabesk* has been a prominent popular-music style. The name itself (the Turkish spelling of the French word *arabesque*) has three interrelated meanings: "in the Arabic style," a highly ornamented musical melody, or a visual design used for Arab and Moorish decorative arts. *Arabesk* shares many musical characteristics (melodic, rhythmic, and arrangement) with 1960s popular-music productions from Syria, Lebanon, and Egypt, but, unlike Arabic popular music, features Anatolian folk instruments, particularly the *bağlama*. Part of the nominal resemblance, however, has to do with the mythical origins of *arabesk* in Southeastern Anatolia, close to the border with Syria. The life stories of *arabesk* singers as portrayed in movies and tabloid articles tell of their birth in the southeast Şanlıurfa region, a poor, working-class life filled with struggles, and overcoming these through moving to Istanbul and becoming employed in the recording and movie industry. This origin myth is so persuasive that *arabesk* has practically become regionalized as if it were the "authentic" local folk music of Şanlıurfa.

According to ethnomusicologist Martin Stokes, *arabesk's* true history differs from the popular origin myths (1992a). The lines between genres—between *arabesk*, *fasıl*, and some arranged Turkish folk-music styles—are fuzzy, as many artists cross over between genres, and there are substantial musical similarities. *Arabesk* melodies are very similar to the *fasıl* melodies performed in *gazino*-s throughout the twentieth century (see Web Resources for examples of *arabesk* videos). All *arabesk* recordings are produced in Istanbul, and the instrumental parts are performed by many of the same studio musicians who also record *türkü*, *şarkı*, and *fasıl*. Furthermore, as in *fasıl*, some *arabesk* singers perform complex gender identities: transgender and transsexual artists Zeki Müren (CD track 16) and Bülent Ersoy, mentioned earlier in relation to *fasıl*, both released numerous *arabesk* albums as well. It is only in *fasıl* and *arabesk* that a significant number of nationally known public performers openly reveal gender identities other than the more socially acceptable heterosexual male and female ones.

Also, not all *arabesk* singers had family origins in rural, Southeastern Anatolia. The first star of the genre, Orhan Gencebay (b. 1944), is from the Black Sea Region; the famous female *arabesk* singer Ebru Gündeş (b. 1974) is from Istanbul, while many respected *fasıl* performers (including employees of the government-sponsored art-music ensembles) with urban roots released *arabesk* recordings. The rural origin myths are more indicative of the long-term urban fascination with rural Anatolia but do not necessarily indicate that there is a tangible musical origin in the traditional local musics of Şanlıurfa.

Arabesk songs typically consist of three sections that repeat in sequence: an instrumental intro, a verse, and a chorus. During the instrumental intros, a variety of instruments may be used: *bağlama* or the *elektrosaz* for the main melody (see below), oud performed in *fasıl* style, or, for more upbeat songs, *zurna* performing *halay*-style dance melodies (Chapter 1). *Arabesk* tends to feature a strong percussion section, typically an ensemble with *darbuka* and *daf* (tambourine) alongside foreign percussion. Many other Anatolian folk instruments appear in the intros to certain *arabesk* songs. *Arabesk* arrangements are in many ways similar to contemporaneous Arabic pop songs, but the diversity of local folk instruments, as well as the distinctive *elektrosaz* sound, distinguish *arabesk* from Arabic pop.

The musical characteristic that most separates *arabesk* from other genres in Turkey is the strong presence of a string orchestra that plays the *cevap* phrases between vocal melodies. The *arabesk* string sound is distinctive and immediately recognizable for several reasons. First, the sound is produced by a small group of string players (typically four to eight violins and violas) who repeatedly overdub the same part, resulting in a simulated orchestra of sixteen to thirty-two musicians. Second, the *arabesk* sound involves sliding between notes and a special kind of slow vibrato unlike any Western classical technique. When this sound is layered, it makes for a very dramatic effect. A small number of string groups are responsible for almost all *arabesk* recordings, meaning that the same musicians can be heard on nearly every *arabesk* album. Currently, the most sought-after string group is Kempa Yaylı Grubu. The best way to experience Kempa is to observe them in action in a recording session. Fortunately, on YouTube, there are numerous clips showing how they do their recording-studio work (search for "Kempa keman" on YouTube. Track 25 [0:08–0:24] features Kempa).

Rock music hit Turkey shortly after its invention in America, and with it came electric guitars, drum set, and electric bass—instruments previously unknown in Turkey. Although Turkish rock has continued to use Western instruments, *arabesk*, as well as the German-Turkish *diskofolk* genre of the 1970s–1980s, was based around a new indigenous instrument: the *elektrosaz*. The three-stringed *elektrosaz* is conceptually similar to a Western electric guitar, although it preserves the shape, movable frets, and picking techniques of the *saz* (Stokes 1992b). There has been considerable experimentation and innovation in *elektrosaz* designs, ranging from the simple application of a piezoelectric pickup to a normal acoustic *bağlama*, to the creation of solid-body instruments with the same string length, but none of the visual aesthetics or timbral quality of the shorter-necked *cura*. Orhan Gencebay's early *arabesk*

recordings featured the *elektrosaz* through phaser and auto-wah gui-tar effect pedals: forty years later this continues to be the quintessen-tial *elektrosaz* sound. *Elektrosaz* is not only used in *arabesk* but also for the performance of the Central Anatolian *misket* dance and other folk dances, and in Alevi sacred/secular music. Cem Karaca became famous for his psychedelic rock covers of Alevi *âşık* repertoire (CD track 6), while Germany-based *diskofolk* group Derdiyoklar performs *âşık* poetry and Alevi *deyiş* on *elektrosaz* and drum set.

Mainstream artists use the term *arabesk* less frequently today. Instead, new stars are marketed as either Turkish pop or "*alaturka*" artists. Musically, there is little difference between *arabesk*, *alaturka*, and Turkish pop, as all share the use of *bağlama* or *elektrosaz* and dramatic string-orchestra *cevap* passages. However, the newer *alaturka* and Turkish pop styles do not emphasize the southeastern origin myths, and they feature more drum machines and synthesizers than an earlier generation of *ara-besk* arrangements.

4.5   KURDISH ARRANGEMENTS AND AYNUR'S "KEÇE KURDAN"

Aynur Doğan (b. 1975) was born in an Alevi-Kurdish village in the Tunceli Province of Turkey and moved to Istanbul in 1992. She studied *türkü* singing and *saz* performance at one of the best-known *dershane*-s (lesson houses) in Istanbul, ASM (Arıf Sağ Müzik). Aynur became best known for her powerful performances in contemporary arrangements of Kurdish-language songs, particularly following her immensely suc-cessful release *Keçe Kurdan* (2004, Kalan Müzik; Figure 4.9). The title track to the album, which translates to "Kurdish girl," became an instant hit in DJed dance clubs. However, two words in the lyrics, *keçê* ("girl") and *ceng* ("battle/fight"), attracted the attention of regional governments, and the municipality of Diyarbakır, the Turkish city with the largest Kurdish-speaking population, banned the CD in 2005 alleging that it encouraged girls to leave their husbands.

Aynur does not perceive or present her music as political in the eth-nic (Kurdish) sense. She performs the Kurdish classical and folk music she grew up hearing because she has the "strongest emotional connec-tion" to it. Her recorded and concert work is not solely Kurdish, as she sings many songs in Turkish and has collaborated with Zaza singer-songwriter Mikaîl Aslan (CD track 26), and she is artistically inspired by "powerful women singers" including Tracy Chapman, PJ Harvey,

FIGURE 4.9   *Aynur.*   *(Courtesy of the Kalan Müzik Archive)*

and Iranian folk singers. She is very vocal for women's issues and international women's rights, which led to an invitation to perform at the WOMAD (World of Music, Arts and Dance) festival in 2008. "Keçe Kurdan" (CD track 25), written by famed Kurdish poet Şivan Perwer, became famous in 1992 with Grup Yorum's cover (see Chapter 5)—it was the first Kurdish recording made in Turkey following the end of a many-decade ban on performing in Kurdish. As in many of the previous arrangements we have examined, the original featured *saz* and vocals and was comparatively simple in arrangement. The song is in the *nim sofyan usulu*, and some sections of the arrangement mimic the feel and sound of *halay* dance music from Southeastern Anatolia. Aynur's singing style has similarities to the

dengbêj and *stranbêj* traditional singing styles (see Yücel 2009, and CD track 27), particularly in her strong delivery and vocal ornaments. One arrangement section references the *arabesk* popular-music style, and others invoke the dramatic spaciousness of film music. The extensive variety of instruments and radical mood changes between song sections are part of the arrangement style of Kemal Sahir Gürel (b. 1966), who also had an active role in arranging Grup Yorum's 1992 recording of the same song. They also reflect the varieties of music recorded at Stüdyo Sound, a studio in Istanbul that specializes in Turkish soap opera and dramatic film scores, and Kurdish folk, pop, and rock album production.

The *arabesk* section of "Keçe Kurdan" (0:08–0:24) features a rapid melody performed on *bağlama* along with Kempa Yaylı Grubu's multitracked and overdubbed string-orchestra parts (Figure 4.10). The repetitive *darbuka* part accentuates "slap" sounds (the sound of the hand slapping and resting on the drumhead) that clearly articulate the *nim sofyan usulu*. An additional percussion part includes echoing bass drum accents (measures 1, 5, 9 and 15) and *djembe*, and assorted objects struck with a stick (measures 13–14). The scalar melodic runs (thoroughly uncharacteristic of any folk- or art-music style or any normal *seyir*-s) and the

FIGURE 4.10   *"Keçe Kurdan" arabesk section. The "percussion" part includes bass drum, djembe, and assorted other percussion. The "melody" part is performed by the string orchestra throughout and doubled by* bağlama *for the first half.*

instrumentation (string orchestra, *bağlama*, and *darbuka* combined) are what define this section as "arabesk."

Immediately following is the *halay* dance section (0:24–0:40; Figure 4.11), where the instrumentation entirely shifts to *zurna* (folk oboe), assorted frame drums, and the *kaval* (end-blown flute). Frame drums now maintain the rhythmic groove (and the *usul* articulation), and gone are the sweeping melodies of the previous section. The *halay* dance melody, derived from the vocal chorus melody, uses a limited number of pitches and features a deep vibrato on the longer, held notes. The *arabesk* section, in contrast, was composed by the arranger and the studio musicians and is not technically part of the song. A different arrangement might have a section similar to this *halay* instrumental section (perhaps extended to create a more continuous dance texture) but would doubtfully have the *arabesk* section as found on Aynur's version.

To match the complex instrumental textures of the song, Aynur's voice is treated in a different way in each vocal section. The first verse (poetry lines one through four, 0:40–1:00) features a single track of Aynur with minimal digital effects processing. The first chorus part

FIGURE 4.11 *"Keçe Kurdan"* halay *dance section. The "melody" part is performed by* zurna, bağlama, *two* kaval *flutes, and electric bass (in different octaves). The "drum" part is performed by several* bendir-s *(frame drums),* erbane-s *(frame drums with hundreds of small rings in the frame), and a* darbuka. *The "tamb." tambourine part plays a straight rhythm that syncopates against the* nim sofyan usulu *emphasized by the various drums.*

(lines five and six, 1:00–1:16), with a melody similar to the preceding *halay* section, features Aynur supported by a male vocal chorus but almost no backing instruments. This suddenly changes in the second chorus part (lines seven through ten, 1:16–1:47), where the heavy frame-drum rhythms return and Aynur's vocal part is doubled and digitally effected, giving a more contemporary "pop" quality to her vocals. The end of the example on the listening CD (from 1:52) is an ethereal section Aynur jokingly described to me as "thousands of Aynurs!" The effect was created through digital delay, where her single vocal improvisation was subjected to dozens of echoes of the original part.

keçê biner çerxa cîhan	Girls get up and announce your voices to the world
zor girêdane me re zor	Difficult things also await you up there
jin çû ne pêş pir dixwînin	Because women are up front and they study now
êdî qelem ket şûna şûr	They take the pen since it's mightier than the sword
keçê em dixwazin bi me re werin şêwrê	Girls, we want you to come into the light with us
dilo em dixwazin bi me re werin cengê	Girls, we want you to come to battle with us
hayê hayê em keçikê kurdan in	Yes, we are Kurdish girls
şêrin em li cengê em li hêviya merdan in	We're lions, we're vivacious, we're the hopes of men
hayê hayê em kulîlkê kurdan in	We are the roses of the Kurds
derdê nezana berbendî serhildan in	We rebelled against the troubles of the ignorant

The Kurdish recording industry had only existed for a few years prior to the release of "Keçe Kurdan." Yet, in this short time, arrangers, studio musicians, and singers had already developed an arrangement style that drew on instrumental folk dance and traditional singing repertoires while incorporating *arabesk,* popular-music idioms, and the latest in digital audio-recording and effects-processing technology.

4.6 PROFILE: ERKAN OĞUR

The history of recorded music in Turkey has, for the most part, consisted of minor revolutions—new combinations of instruments, new combinations of previously separate genres, and new ways of articulating the core musical aspects of Anatolian music. Occasionally, major revolutions—radical breaks from previous ways of making music— have resulted in the quick adoption of a completely new musical sound. Erkan Oğur (b. 1954), a multi-instrumentalist, singer, composer, instrument builder, and arranger, is particularly noteworthy in this regard. His professional musical background includes 1960s psychedelic rock, jazz and blues, Turkish-language folk musics from numerous regions (particularly from his hometown of Elazığ), Klasik Türk Müziği, and collaborations with numerous popular musicians. Erkan is famous for demanding exacting precision with every single note that is recorded, both his own playing and that of other musicians contributing to the same song. Erkan has recorded with many musicians, including Dertli Divani, Şevval Sam, Fatih Yaşar, Kardeş Türküler, and Sezen Aksu.

 At a time when staged performances of *türkü* were steadily becoming faster, louder, and denser, Erkan Oğur, along with Rize-born singer İsmail Hakkı Demircioğlu (b. 1957), strove for the opposite aesthetic, creating the slowest, most delicate, and most spacious recordings of *türkü* (CD track 8). The duo popularized a large amount of once esoteric repertoire, particularly *âşık* poetry, *destan türküsü*, and Alevi *deyiş*. Most striking, at first, are the instrumental sounds of his recordings, as Erkan has invented several new instruments. His *perdesiz gitar* is inspired by the nylon-stringed classical guitar. Fretless guitars have been made by American and European luthiers in the past, but Erkan's *perdesiz gitar* has a distinctive tone quality and performing style that draws more on Turkish classical *tanbur* and oud technique and ornamentation than on any Western guitar picking or strumming technique. You can hear the *perdesiz gitar* performing the instrumental melody for the Elazığ *türküsü* "Çayın Öte Yüzünde" (CD track 28), and a jazz improvisation on the same instrument (CD track 29). (Also search on YouTube for numerous videos of Erkan Oğur with his *perdesiz gitar*.) Erkan's other well-known invention is the *kopuz* (Figure 4.12)—a reconstruction of the Central Asian three-stringed lute widely believed to be the ancestor of all *saz*-family instruments. Erkan often uses the *kopuz* to play intricate finger-picked *cevap* phrases, or bright-sounding strummed chords (CD track 8).

Other instrument makers have also invented new instruments or modified existing ones, but there is something particularly noteworthy to

FIGURE 4.12   *Erkan Oğur playing* kopuz.   *(Courtesy of the Kalan Müzik Archive)*

Erkan's above two inventions. The *perdesiz gitar* has practically become a new Anatolian folk instrument, as many musicians now imitate Erkan's sound, which is not based on classical or electric guitar technique but rather on Anatolian folk and art instrument technique. The *kopuz* is interesting, since this newly invented instrument is a re-creation of a medieval Central Asian lute, and the technique that Erkan developed has little in common with instrument playing styles found in Turkey today but much in common with Central Asian Turkic lute techniques. Erkan's recordings and performances, on the one hand, bring Turkish folk music into a previously unexplored timbral realm (the use of guitar), and on the other, bring the aesthetics closer to the mythological, medieval Central Asian origins of Turkish music.

4.7   CONCLUSION

Arrangement, as a form of musical practice, does not exist solely in Turkey, but in Turkey there is a clear link between recorded and performed arrangements and the continued vitality of folk and art musics. As we have seen, many of the basic structures of the music remain intact, including concepts of musical time (*usul*), musical mode (*makam*), melodic shape (*seyir*), and vocal and instrumental ornamentation styles. In Turkey, a staggering variety of instruments are used in arrangements, yet certain instruments have such strong connotations that they have come to symbolize a region or locality itself, as is the case with the *Karadeniz kemençe* (symbolizing the Eastern Black Sea Region) and the *klasik kemençe* (symbolizing the Aegean Region). In "ethnic" arrangement styles such as Kazım Koyuncu's and Marsis's "Laz rock," the practice of arrangement only began in the 1990s. However, arranged Laz music quickly became instrumental for the emergent Laz youth movement in the Eastern Black Sea and in migrant Laz communities in Istanbul, Ankara, and other large cities. The arrangement of rural, folkloric practices within modern, urban soundscapes thus parallels other, nonmusical aspects of Laz youth life. More generally, contemporary arrangements in Turkey draw on elements of Anatolian rural folk musics, urban art music, *and* foreign influences, which effectively blurs the lines between "folk," "art," and "popular" music styles.

CHAPTER 5

Music, Politics, and Meaning

I have pursued the theme of how music in Turkey continues to be an integral part of national identity and the formation of a national consciousness about local and regional cultural differences. I have also explored how studio and stage arrangement practices have been of key importance to this endeavor. In this chapter, I look more explicitly at cultural politics by examining three instances when music became inseparable from politics and came to symbolize significant political debates or events themselves.

5.1 IN MEMORY OF A GENERAL: ÂŞIK VEYSEL'S "ATATÜRK'E AĞIT"

Âşık Veysel Şatıroğlu (1894–1973) is considered the first "modern âşık," and his recordings had a major influence on the dissemination of *âşık* folk poetry through audio recordings and radio (Figure 5.1). Unlike previous generations of *âşık* poets from Sivas (Chapter 1), Veysel was not a wandering minstrel (although he did travel and perform across the country), and he did not become known through traditional *âşık* competitions. Instead, he was "discovered" at the first Sivas *âşık* festival in 1931. His composed *deyiş*, and those of other *âşık*-s that he sang, were in an older village style and often thematically pertained to village life.

Like many *âşık*-s, Âşık Veysel was politically minded. During the 1940s, he performed at events for the CHP (Republican People's Party), founded by Mustafa Kemal Atatürk as Turkey's first political party. Âşık Veysel had met Atatürk numerous times, and following Atatürk's death in 1938, he composed "Atatürk'e Ağıt" (Lament for Atatürk) to honor the life and deeds of the founder of the Turkish Republic. Following its release, this was the top-selling recording in Turkey, and to this day it continues to be regularly played on the radio. Every November 10, the

FIGURE 5.1 *Âşık Veysel playing the* saz. *(Courtesy of the Kalan Müzik Archive)*

anniversary of Atatürk's death, town and city governments play this recording (CD track 3).

"Atatürk'e Ağıt" uses an eight-syllable rhyming pattern, so some word choices were made in the interest of preserving the rhyming sequence. This means that, unfortunately, much of the meaning and sentiment of this ballad is lost in translation. You can at least gain a sense of the themes chosen by Âşık Veysel—he credits Atatürk with trains, airplanes, armies, and modern urban development, referring to him twice as "God's lion" (*Tanrı'nın aslanı*). He also refers to İnönü İsmet (1884–1973), a Turkish army general who became the second president of the Republic of Turkey, and Mustafa Fevzi Çakmak (1876–1950), an army marshal and prime minister of Turkey.

Atatürk'ün eserleri	*Atatürk's works*
Söylenecek bundan geri	*It will be said that from now on*
Bütün dünyanın her yeri	*Everywhere around the world bore [this grief]*
Ah çekti vatan ağladı	*Everyone in the land cried*
Fabrikalar icad etti	*He invented factories*
Atalığın ispat etti	*Proof of his fatherliness*

Varlığın Türk'e terk etti	*He left his being to the Turks*
Döndü çark devran ağladı	*The wheel of fortune spun, the streams of time cried*
Bu ne kuvvet bu ne kudret	*What power is this, what might*
Varıdı bunda bir hikmet	*There was wisdom in all this*
Bütün Türkler İnönü İsmet	*İnönü İsmet, the eyes of all Turks*
Gözlerinden kan ağladı	*Have shed tears of blood*
Tren hattı tayyareler	*Train lines to planes*
Türkler giydi hep kareler	*Turks are now wearing only black*
Semerkand'ı Buhara'lar	*Samarkand, Bukhara heard of it*
İşitti her yan ağladı	*Everywhere cried*
Siz sağ olun Türk gençleri	*Turkish youth, say thanks*
Çalışanlar kalmaz geri	*The workers will not remain undeveloped*
Mareşal Fevzi'nin askerleri	*Marshal Fevzi's soldiers*
Ordular teğmen ağladı	*and the armies and lieutenants cried*
Zannetme ağlayan gülmez	*Do not think the criers do not laugh*
Aslan yatağı boş kalmaz	*The lion's bed will not remain empty*
Yalınız gidenler gelmez	*Those who go alone will not come*
Felek-el mevt'in elinden	*Destiny's hand, from the hand of the dying*
Her gelen insan ağladı	*All people who come have cried*
Uzatma Veysel bu sözü	*Don't lengthen these words, Veysel*
Dayanmaz herkesin özü	*Everyone's essence cannot bear*
Koruyalım yurdumuzu	*Let's protect our homeland*
Dost değil düşman ağladı	*Not the friend: it was the enemy who cried*

5.2 FOLK HEROES AND SOCIALIST POLITICS IN THE SONGS OF GRUP YORUM

For twenty-five years, Grup Yorum have been at the forefront of a genre known as *protest* or *özgün* ("authentic") music. *Protest*, as a style, combines the rhythms and instruments of *türkü* with elements of

American rock, international socialist marches, and Latin American political music. Although they do perform anonymously authored *türkü, oyun havaları*, and authored Alevi *deyiş*, Grup Yorum are best known for collectively authoring several hundred new compositions. In their *protest* songs, they advocate for prisoner's rights, sing against imperialism and capitalism, and decry the atrocities of war. They received notoriety in 1988 for openly performing a song in the Kurdish language, which was illegal at the time and resulted in the imprisonment of the group. When the language ban was lifted in 1991, their recording of the song "Keçê Kurdan" was one of the first arranged songs in Kurdish to be released on the Turkish market. Their political activism, which extends beyond the stage to participating in organized protests and antiwar marches around Turkey, has resulted in many members of the group being repeatedly jailed and some becoming permanently exiled outside of Turkey. Their musical activity includes not just controversial Kurdish songs but numerous folk songs in Turkish, Zazaki, and other Anatolian ethnic languages, and songs popular in the international socialist movement, such as "Bella Ciao."

Despite a blanket ban on airing Grup Yorum recordings on radio or TV and regional bans on the sale of their albums, Yorum have been one of the top-selling musical groups in Turkey of any genre, selling over ten million albums combined. For their fans, Yorum are the voice of Turkey's active revolutionary socialist movement. One translation of the word *yorum* is "commentary," and the songs Grup Yorum sing are a substantial commentary on how contemporary Turkey is polarized around issues of ethnic rights, political democracy, and Turkey's for-eign, domestic, and military policy.

In the song "Kavuşma" (CD track 30), Grup Yorum sing about two legendary figures, Börklüce and Çakırcalı. Börklüce Mustafa (d. 1416) was a leader of one of the only indigenous armed uprisings against the Ottoman sultanate, which transpired in the Karaburun area near present-day Izmir (on the Aegean coast). He hoped to democratize land-ownership rights and liberate the citizens of Karaburun from oppressive taxes. The revolution was ultimately unsuccessful (and led to his crucifixion), but Börklüce became a folk hero for standing up for the rights of the poor and oppressed. Çakırcalı Mehmet Efe (1872–1910) was a Zeybek Efe (bandit leader from the mountainous regions above Izmir) and, like Börklüce, became a folk hero for fighting to bring justice to poor citizens of the Aegean area.

İnsanoğlu vura öle	*Mankind keeps shooting and killing*
Gece güne döne döne	*The night keeps turning into day*
Tutuşmaz mı bu karanlık	*Can this darkness not ignite*
En yiğitler yana yana	*The most brave keep on burning*
Şen olasın anacığım	*May you be joyous, oh my mother*
Oğlun erdi muradına	*Your son attained his desire*
Destan oldu vatanına...	*Became a legend for your homeland...*
Pir Sultan soyundan akan yiğitler	*From Pir Sultan's lineage flows brave young men*
Börklüce'yle cenge kalkan yiğitler	*Brave men who rise up to battle with Börkluce*
Çakırcalı'dan beri konaklar yakıp yıkan	*Ever since Çakırcalı, brave men burned and destroyed villas*
Zulmün bileğini büken yiğitler	*They can overpower oppression*

Zeybek dance songs often sing about legendary outlaws such as Çakırcalı, and Grup Yorum arranged "Kavuşma" in a *zeybek* style, with *askı-davul* and *bağlama* played in an Aegean regional style. However, the piece is not a traditional *zeybek*, and their arrangement uses non-traditional instruments including oboe and electric bass. Yorum frequently mix traditional folk-song styles and instruments with new sounds, and they have a penchant for relating contemporary geopolitical struggles to folk legends and Anatolian history. Although many of Yorum's fans are not native to the Aegean but rather to other parts of Turkey, heroes such as Çakırcalı have become nationally known while retaining their regional associations, and are championed as examples of inspirational leaders for a young generation of revolutionary socialist activists.

5.3 AZERI AND ARMENIAN IDENTITY AND THE STORY OF "SARI GELİN/SARİ GYALİN"

There is perhaps no song in Anatolia with a more contested meaning than "Sarı Gelin" (Armenian: Sari Gyalın). Versions of the song exist in the Azeri, Armenian, Kurdish, and Turkish languages. Even the song title is contested: *sarı gelin* in Turkish translates to "yellow bride" or "blond-haired bride," while the word *sari* (note the dotted *i*) in Western

Armenian means "highlander," not "yellow." Regardless of the version or language, the song sings of an impossible love, typically implying one between a Christian and a Muslim. More recently, the song has titled two war-related movies, and became symbolic of the plight of the Armenian minority of Turkey. Present known versions of the song are almost certainly local to Erzurum, an Eastern Anatolian city that prior to World War I was known for its ethnic diversity.

"Sari Gyalin," first verse, in Armenian (as sung by Kardeş Türküler) (CD track 31)

Ambela para para	*The clouds bit by bit*
Neynim aman, neynim aman, sari gyalin	*Highlander bride*
Yes im siradzin çara	*I couldn't take my beloved*
Akh, merıt merni, sari gyalin, dardod yarim	*Ah, let your mother die, highlander bride*

"Sarı Gəlin," first verse, in Azeri (CD track 32)

Saçın ucun hörməzlər	*You don't braid the end of your hair*
Gülü sulu dərməzlər, Sarı gəlin	*You don't pick a wet rose, yellow bride*
Bu sevda nə sevdadır	*This love, what kind of love is this*
Səni mənə verməzlər	*You won't be given to me*
Neynim aman, aman, Sarı gəlin	*Oh, oh, yellow bride*

"Sari Gelin" (1999) is the title of an Azeri movie drama about the 1980s Armenian-Azeri military conflict and the development of an unexpected friendship between an Armenian and an Azeri soldier. The film, the first made in the independent republic of Azerbaijan following the end of Soviet rule, invoked the song "Sari Gelin" and the image of a bride in yellow to symbolically depict death and the cruelty of fate. Even prior to the movie release, the song had held a special significance amongst Azeris in connection with the Armenian-Azeri war. In 2008, the Turkish military funded a documentary about the Armenian-Turkish conflict of 1915 entitled "Sarı Gelin." In contrast to the Azeri film, the Turkish documentary received notoriety from lawsuits stemming from its gruesome images, its mandatory inclusion in elementary school history curricula, and a widespread concern that the movie would lead to continued harassment and murders of ethnically Armenian Turkish citizens.

More than any other event, for many in Turkey the song is indelibly linked with the murder of Armenian journalist Hrant Dink (1954–2007) and the funeral march that took place in Istanbul on January 23, 2007. Hrant Dink had been brought to trial three times under the infamous Turkish Penal Code Article 301, which makes it a crime to insult the Turkish government, governmental institutions, or the Turkish ethnicity. Typically, "301 charges" are brought against those who publicly proclaim or write about the mandatory relocation of Armenians that transpired in 1915 as a "genocide," a categorization of the action that is denied by Turkey and several of its allies but recognized by the Council of Europe, numerous countries, and nongovernmental organizations. Ironically, of all the prominent Armenian journalists, Dink was one of the least vocal about the events of 1915. During his life he worked principally towards creating a greater dialogue between the Turkish and Armenian communities of Turkey, and between the countries of Turkey and Armenia. However, having had 301 charges brought against him made him a political target. He received over two thousand death threats and ultimately was assassinated by members of an ultra-right-wing nationalist group.

Over one hundred thousand mourners marched the five-mile stretch from the offices of the *Agos* newspaper, where Hrant Dink had been the editor-in-chief, to his gravesite in Yenikapı (Figure 5.2). For the most part, the marchers were completely silent. However, most of the marchers were not ethnically Armenian. By recent estimates, only fifty thousand Armenians are presently citizens of Turkey. The funeral march was striking due to the outpouring from numerous ethnic communities—Turks, Kurds, Zazas, and Armenians carried the same signs, a show of solidarity against fascism and ethnic intolerance that targeted Hrant Dink (and numerous other journalists before him).

Although the marchers were silent, one sound accompanied the five-mile march: "Sari Gyalin." The Kardeş Türküler version sung in Armenian (CD track 31) and the instrumental version played by Armenian *duduk* player Jivan Gasparyan were repeatedly broadcast from a van that traveled the funeral march route. Since that historic day, the meaning of "Sarı Gelin," a song that already had intense meanings, intensified even further.

FIGURE 5.2   *The funeral march for Hrant Dink. The signs say "Hepimiz Hrant Dink'iz/Hepimiz Ermeniyiz" (We all are Hrant Dink/We all are Armenians). There are also signs written in Armenian ("Menk Polorys Hay Enk") and in Kurmancı ("Em Henû Hrantin").*   (Photo by Eliot Bates)

"Sarı Gelin"—the song today conjures memories of bitter wars, of assassinations, of interethnic violence. Yet in the very same song, the singer mourns for their love, the love of a woman of another ethnicity. For longer than there has been ethnically related violence in Anatolia, there has been love that crossed those cultural boundaries.

Afterword

∞

My intent in this book has been to show the many kinds of connections between the musical, the social, and the technological in contemporary Turkey. I chose to focus on Istanbul, a metropolis with a vibrant musical culture that has been profoundly influenced by a long history of urban art- and folk-music making and (more recently) by the musics brought by waves of migrants from nearly every locality in rural Anatolia. In the words of musician Orhan Gencebay, "Istanbul, köylerin birleşimi olan bir yerdir" (Istanbul is a place where villages come together) (Akkaya and Çelik 2006, 246).

One theme in this book has been the formation of a national consciousness about regional and local cultural differences. The fervor for collecting local folk songs extends back to the 1930s, when folklore collection was an essential part of the development of a national culture. Government-ensemble performances shortly thereafter helped to disseminate this repertoire but did so in a way that both reified the concept of discrete cultural regions (e.g., Aegean, Central Anatolia) and preserved a sense of musical differences. The privatization of the music industry and establishment of Unkapanı as the center for the Turkish recording industry happened simultaneously with a mass emigration from rural Anatolia to Istanbul, and many entrepreneurial record labels opened up to cater to the emerging markets for local musics. In the 1990s, new labels explored Anatolian ethnic-language markets, leading to an explosion of activity in the production of Kurdish, Lazuri, Zazaki, and other language musics.

I discussed the social nature of music in Turkey in relation to pedagogical contexts and audience-performer interactions, another book theme. For some musical practices, traditional informal performance contexts (such as Alevi *muhabbet*) continue to be important but are now supplemented by group classes that transpire in private lesson houses. In other musical practices, the shutting down of traditional sites (such as the Enderun school and Mevlevi lodges) was followed by the emergence of neighborhood music associations, oud workshops, and Western-style conservatories as the most important sites for pedagogy.

Finally, rural- and urban-origin music practices have continued to have a strong vitality in twenty-first-century Turkey, which I explored in relation to two themes: the long-standing practice of arranging repertoire, and the ongoing prominence of Anatolian instruments in contemporary music making. Arrangements today are made for either stage performances or multitrack digital audio recordings. In both cases, the presence of traditional Anatolian instruments, ranging from those local to one village to those found nationwide, is essential for keeping the music rooted in concepts of locality, region, and nation. Arrangement also extends the sound world of music in Turkey, as cutting-edge digital audio techniques are now part of the creation of all musical styles, and foreign instruments have been adapted for the performance of rural and urban musics.

Glossary

ağır aksak "slow limp"; a four-beat *usul* (short+short+short+long, or long+short+short+short) notated in $\frac{9}{4}$ or $\frac{9}{2}$

aksak "limp"; 1) any asymmetrical *usul*; 2) a four-beat *usul* (short+short+short+long, or long+short+short+short) notated in $\frac{9}{8}$

aksak semai a four-beat *usul* (long+short+short+long) notated in $\frac{10}{4}$ or $\frac{10}{8}$

Alevi a hereditary heterodox sect related to Bektaşi Sufism, Sh'ia Islam, and the Iranian Ah-le Haqq; Kurdish-, Turkish-, and Zazaki-speaking Alevis traditionally lived in rural Anatolia

Anatolia the West Asian subcontinent located within the borders of the Republic of Turkey

arabesk a popular-music genre in Turkey

arrangement the process of orchestrating rural- and art-music repertoire for performing ensembles or recording-studio productions

âşık "in love"; a folk poet who composes poetry and songs, and typically performs *saz*

âyîn a suite form in Mevlevi Sufi music

bağlama long-necked lute with movable frets and three courses of strings (a total of three to eight strings) found in Turkey; see also *saz*

bendir frame drum without cymbals or rattles

beat structure see *usul*

bozlak an *uzun hava* style sung by *âşık*-s of Central Anatolia

cem Alevi sacred ceremony

cemevi Alevi worship house, or a space converted for the purposes of hosting a *cem* ceremony

cemiyet community association

cevap (also: *ara-saz*) answer phrase

109

chromaticism melodic style using all twelve Western pitches within an octave

curcuna see *aksak semai*

darbuka goblet-shaped drum

davul "drum" (performer of: *davulcu*); also, *askı-davul, asma-davul*: double-headed drum played with one large mallet and a thin stick

dede religious leader of Alevi *cem* ceremonies

dengbêj Kurdish male epic singer

dernek private club where music lessons are given

dershane private lesson house for group music classes

destan an *uzun hava* style with epic poetic themes, found in Eastern Anatolia and the Eastern Black Sea

devr-i hindi a three-beat *usul* (short+short+long) notated in $\frac{7}{8}$

devr-i turan a three-beat *usul* (long+short+short) notated in $\frac{7}{8}$

deyiş genre of slow-tempo Alevi composed song used in secular and sacred contexts

düm a syllable representing the lowest sound possible on a drum

durak "resting place"; the final note of a musical work, and a defining note of a *makam*

Eastern Anatolia a region in Turkey extending from the province of Malatya to the Iranian and Azerbaijani borders

Eastern Black Sea a region in northeastern Turkey encompassing the provinces of Giresun, Trabzon, Rize, and Artvin

editing the stage in recording production after the actual recording of instruments but before mixing

elektrosaz a three-stringed electric instrument based on the *bağlama* or *cura-saz*

embellishment notes added to the principal melody

fasıl 1) a suite form in Klasik Türk Müziği; 2) performance of TSM in a *gazino* or *meyhane* context

gazino upper-class urban nightclub featuring *fasıl* performance

hafız one who has memorized the Qur'an

halay two-step line dances of Central, Eastern and Southeastern Anatolia with music in the *nim sofyan usulu*, typically performed by a *davul-zurna* ensemble *hasbıhâl* see *muhabbet*

Hemşin a Muslim-Armenian ethnicity living in the mountainous Eastern Black Sea Region

heterorhythmic a texture derived from multiple layers, each performing different embellished rhythms based on the same beat structure

horon line dances done in the Black Sea Region, most commonly involving music in *Türk aksağı, devr-i turan,* and *devr-i hindi usulu* that is performed on the *kemençe, tulum,* or *kaval*; related to the Bulgarian *horo*

kanun (performer of: *kanuni*) plucked box zither with twenty-six courses of strings

kaval end-blown reed flute used for performing rural Anatolian folk music

kemençe (Greek: *Pontos lyra*; performer of: *kemençeci*) three-stringed bowed box lute played in the Eastern Black Sea Region and historically primarily performed by Laz and Pontic Greeks

karşılama a partner dance found in the Thracian and Aegean Regions with music in a fast *aksak usulu* ($\frac{9}{8}$)

klasik kemençe (Greek: *politiki lyra*) three-stringed pear-shaped bowed lute played in the Aegean Region, and in urban art musics since the late nineteenth century

kırık hava "broken air"; a genre of *türkü* encompassing metered folk songs

Klasik Türk Müziği Classical Turkish music of the Ottoman era, including urban instrumental art music and vocal music in Osmanlıca

kopuz the Central Asian long-necked lute believed to be the ancestor of the modern *saz*

Laz an ethnicity living along the Eastern Black Sea coast

Lazuri a language in the South Caucasian language family spoken by the Laz of Turkey and Georgia

longa instrumental urban art-music form primarily in the *nim sofyan usulu*

makam (plural: *makamlar*) melodic modes used in urban art music and in some rural folk-music traditions

memleket ancestral homeland

meşk a traditional context for urban art-music pedagogy and performance involving instruments being passed around a group of musicians of differing ages and competences

meter regular grouping of beats

Mevlevi Sufi religious order founded by the followers of Jalal ad-Din Rumi

meyhane urban restaurant that serves liquor and features live *fasıl* or *türkü* performance

misket folk dance from Ankara and Central Anatolia with music in *nim sofyan usulu*

mixing the stage in recording production that results in a completed rendition of a musical work

modulation shifting between one melodic mode and another

muhabbet 1) in Alevi culture, a gathering featuring a conversation created through shared songs; 2) in Central Anatolia, *muhabbet gecesi* are social music-filled evenings featuring dance

ney (performer of: *neyzen*) end-blown reed flute used for performing Mevlevi Sufi music and Klasik Türk Müziği

nim sofyan a three-beat *usul* (long+long+short) notated in $\frac{8}{8}$

Osmanlıca Ottoman Turkish language, written primarily with a modified Arabic script; the official administrative language until 1928

oud (performer of: *'ûdi*) short-necked fretless plucked lute with eleven strings

oyun havası a genre of *türkü* encompassing instrumental dance music

perdesiz gitar a fretless guitar invented by Erkan Oğur in the 1970s

peşrev an instrumental urban art music form utilizing long, complex rhythmic meters

polyrhythmic a texture derived from multiple layers, each performing distinct rhythms

prescriptive notation minimalist notation that gives instructions on how to sound out the music

protest (also: *özgün*) leftist political music genre

rakı grape-seed liquor

raksan a six-beat *usul* (long+long+short+short+short+long) notated in $\frac{15}{8}$

Roman an ethnicity originally of Central Asian origin that now lives throughout Europe and West Asia. Most of the Rom in Turkey are Muslim and of the Xoraxane ethnicity.

saz "instrument"; a family of long-necked lutes with movable frets and three courses of strings (a total of three to eight strings) found in Turkey; members of the *saz* family, ranging from the shortest to longest *tekne* (faces) include: *cura, dedesaz, tambura, bağlama, çöğür,* and *divan*

saz semaisi instrumental urban art-music form primarily in the *aksak semai usulu*

sema the ritual movement done in Mevlevi Sufi ceremonies

semah a ritual dance traditionally performed in Alevi *cemevi*-s by couples; more recently, a staged dance for Alevi concert performances

seyir melodic contour; a defining feature of a particular *makam*

soru question

Southeastern Anatolia a region in Turkey with provinces that border on Syria and Iraq

şarkı "song"; primary vocal-music genre of TSM

şelpe finger-picking and fingernail-strumming techniques used in some *saz*-playing styles, particularly for playing the smaller *cura* and *dedesaz*

syncopation musical accents that occur between beats

tanbur (performer of: *tanburi*) long-necked lute with seven or eight strings and movable frets, used primarily in Ottoman court music (The Ottoman *tanbur* should not be confused with unrelated instruments sharing the same name. The Anatolian *tambura* is a medium-sized *saz*, the Indian *tambura* is an instrument with a gourd resonator used for drone accompaniment, and the eastern European *tamboura/tamburica* looks like a cross between a guitar and a *saz*.)

tek a syllable representing a contrasting, high-pitched drum sound

tezene 1) a flexible, short pick used for playing the *saz*; 2) *saz*-playing style incorporating a pick *tulum* (performer of: *tulumcu*)   bagpipe found only in mountainous villages of the Eastern Black Sea with a double chanter and no drone pipe

Türk aksağı   a two-beat *usul* (short+long) notated in $\frac{5}{8}$ or $\frac{5}{4}$

TSM (Türk Sanat Müziği)   urban art music with lyrics in the Turkish language

türkü   Turkish-language folk songs of unknown authorship; see also *kırık hava, oyun havası, uzun hava*

usul   a named, ordered pattern of long and short beats that defines the metrical structure of a musical piece

uzun hava   "long air"; a genre of *türkü* encompassing semi-improvised nonmetrical songs

Yörük   nomadic Turkic tribe living in mountainous regions of Turkey

Zaza   an ethnicity that lives in Eastern Anatolia

Zazaki (also: Dimli)   a language in the Zazaki-Gorani branch of the Northwest Iranian language family spoken by Zazas

zeybek   a slow, male solo or circle dance done in the Aegean Region, commonly involving music in *ağır aksak usulu* that is performed on the *bağlama* or *zurna* and accompanied by *davul*

zurna   an Anatolian folk oboe

References

Ahrens, Christian. 1973. "Polyphony in *Touloum* Playing by the Pontic Greeks." *Yearbook of the International Folk Music Council* 5:122–31.

Akkaya, Ayhan and Fehmiye Çelik. 2006. *60'lardan 70'lere...45'lik Şarkılar* (From the 60s to the 70s...45 Rpm Songs). Istanbul: BGST Yayınları.

Aksoy, Bülent. 2005. "On These Recordings," from the liner notes to *Masters of Turkish Music: Kemençe*. Kalan Müzik, Istanbul.

Andrews, Peter A. 1989. *Ethnic Groups in the Republic of Turkey*. Wiesbaden: Reichert.

Bartók, Béla. 2002 [1976]. *Turkish Folk Music from Asia Minor*. Homosassa, FL: Bartok Records.

Bates, Eliot. 2008. "Social Interactions, Musical Arrangement, and the Production of Digital Audio in Istanbul Recording Studios." Ph.D. Dissertation, University of California, Berkeley.

———. 2010. "Mixing for *Parlak* and Bowing for a *Büyük Ses*: The Aesthetics of Arranged Traditional Music in Turkey." *Ethnomusicology* 54(1):81–105.

Beken, Münir. 1998. "Musicians, Audience and Power: The Changing Aesthetics at the Maksim Gazino of Istanbul." Ph.D. Dissertation, University of Maryland.

Bryant, Wanda. 1991. "Musical Change in Turkish Zurna Music." *Pacific Review of Ethnomusicology* 6:1–34.

Erdener, Yıldıray. 1995. *The Song Contests of Turkish Minstrels: Improvised Poetry Sung to Traditional Music*. London: Taylor and Francis.

Feldman, Walter. 1996. *Music of the Ottoman Court: Makam, Composition and the Early Ottoman Instrumental Repertoire*. Berlin: Verlag für Wissenschaft und Bildung.

Göksel, Aslı and Celia Kerslake. 2005. *Turkish: A Comprehensive Grammar*. London: Routledge.

Göktürk, Yücel. 2009. "İncelir ama kopmaz bu yol" (A Path That Is Thinning But Will Not Break Off). *Roll Dergisi* (October 1). http://www.ulasozdemir. com/pressDetail.php?lang=Tr&pressSub=2009&pg=6&pressId=42

Hooshmandrad, Partow. 2004. "Performing the Belief: Sacred Musical Practice of the Kurdish Ahl-i Haqq of Gūrān." Ph.D. Dissertation, University of California, Berkeley.

Kalaycıoğlu, Can and Feryal Öney. 2007. "Dertli Divanî, Ulaş Özdemir ve Ahmet Koçak ile 'Hasbıhâl' Eyledik" (Making Conversation with Dertli Divani, Ulaş Özdemir and Ahmet Koçak). *BGST Müzik*, http://www.bgst.org/muzik/yazilar/hasbihal.asp

Karakaya, Fikret. 2005. "History of *Kemençe*," from the liner notes to *Masters of Turkish Music: Kemençe*. Kalan Müzik, Istanbul.

Klaser, Rajna. 2001. "From an Imagined Paradise to an Imagined Nation: Interpreting *Şarkı* as a Cultural Play." Ph.D. Dissertation, University of California, Berkeley.

Lewis, Geoffrey. 1999. *The Turkish Language Reform: A Catastrophic Success.* New York: Oxford University Press.

Marcus, Scott L. 2007. *Music in Egypt: Experiencing Music, Expressing Culture.* New York: Oxford University Press.

Markoff, Irene. 1986a. "Musical Theory, Performance and the Contemporary *Bağlama* Specialist in Turkey." Ph.D. Dissertation, University of Washington.

———. 1986b. "The Role of Expressive Culture in the Demystification of a Secret Sect of Islam: The Case of the Alevis of Turkey." *The World of Music* 28:42–56.

———. 1990. "The Ideology of Musical Practice and the Professional Turkish Folk Musician: Tempering the Creative Impulse." *Asian Music* 22(1): 129–45.

———. 2002a. "Alevi Identity and Expressive Culture." In *Garland Encyclopedia of World Music, Volume 6: The Middle East*, ed. V. Danielson, S. Marcus, and D. Reynolds. New York: Routledge, 793–800.

———. 2002b. "Aspects of Turkish Folk Music Theory." In *Garland Encyclopedia of World Music, Volume 6: The Middle East*, ed. V. Danielson, S. Marcus, and D. Reynolds. New York: Routledge, 77–88.

Onat, Aslı. 2008. "Bu albümlerde 'hâl' var" (There's a State to This Album). *Milliyet* Sanat (August 1), 30–31. http://www.ulasozdemir.com/pressDetail.php?lang=Tr&pressSub=2008&pg=6&pressId=18

O'Connell, John Morgan. 2002. "Snapshot: Tanburi Cemil Bey." In *Garland Encyclopedia of World Music, Volume 6: The Middle East*, ed. V. Danielson, S. Marcus, and D. Reynolds. New York: Routledge, 757–58.

Öztuna, Yılmaz. 2006. *Türk Mûsikîsi: Akademik Klasik Türk San'at Mûsikîsi'nin Ansiklopedik Sözlüğü* (Turkish Music: An Encyclopedic Dictionary of Academic Classical Turkish Art Music). Ankara: Orient Yayınları.

Öztürk, Okan Murat. 2004. *Zeybek Kültürü ve Müziği* (Zeybek Culture and Music). Istanbul: Pan Yayıncılık.

Picken, Laurence Ernest Rowland. 1975. *Folk Musical Instruments of Turkey.* London: Oxford University Press.

Popescu-Judetz, Eugenia. 1999. *Prince Dimitrie Cantemir: Theorist and Composer of Turkish Music*. Istanbul: Pan Yayıncılık.

Redhouse Yayınevi. 2004. *Redhouse Büyük Elsözlüğü* (The Larger Redhouse Portable Dictionary), 20th printing. Istanbul: Redhouse Yayınevi.

Seeman, Sonia Tamar. 2002. "'You're Roman!' Musical Practice and Social Identity in Turkish Roma Communities." Ph. D. Dissertation, University of California, Los Angeles.

———. 2006. "Presenting 'Gypsy', Re-Representing Roman: Towards an Archeology of Aesthetic Production and Social Identity." *Music and Anthropology* 11.

Shiloah, Amnon. 1993. "An Eighteenth-Century Critic of Taste and Good Taste." In *Ethnomusicology and Modern Music History*, edited by S. Blum and D. Neuman. Urbana: University of Illinois Press, 181–89. (article about Charles Fonton)

Signell, Karl. 1977. *Makam: Modal Practice in Turkish Art Music*. Seattle: Asian Music Publications.

Sökefeld, Martin. 2008. *Struggling for Recognition: The Alevi Movement in Germany and Transnational Space*. New York: Berghahn Books.

Stokes, Martin. 1992a. *The Arabesk Debate: Music and Musicians in Modern Turkey*. Oxford: Clarendon Press.

———. 1992b. "The Media and Reform: The *Saz* and *Elektrosaz* in Urban Turkish Folk Music." *British Journal of Ethnomusicology* 1:89–103.

———. 2002. "Turkish Rock and Pop." In *Garland Encyclopedia of World Music, Volume 6: The Middle East*, ed. V. Danielson, S. Marcus, and D. Reynolds. New York: Routledge, 247–54.

van Bruinessen, Martin. 1996. "Kurds, Turks and the Alevi Revival." *Middle Eastern Reports* 200, 7–10.

Vicente, Victor. 2007. "The Aesthetics of Motion in Musics for the Mevlana Celal ed-Din Rumi." Ph.D. Dissertation, University of Maryland.

Yurdatapan, Şanar. 2004. "Turkey: Censorship Past and Present." In *Shoot the Singer! Music Censorship Today*, ed. M. Korpe. London: Zed Books, 189–96.

Yücel, Clémence Scalbert. 2009. "The Invention of a Tradition: Diyarbakır's Dengbêj Project." *European Journal of Turkish Studies* 10.

Resources

Additional Reading

Başgöz, İlhan. 2008. *Hikâye: Turkish Folk Romance as Performance Art.* Bloomington: Indiana University Press.

Beken, Münir. 2003. "Aesthetics and Artistic Criticism at the Turkish Gazino." *Music and Anthropology* 8.

Blum, Stephen, and Amir Hassanpour. 1996. "'The Morning of Freedom Rose Up': Kurdish Popular Song and the Exigencies of Cultural Survival." *Popular Music* 15(3):325–43.

Kendal, Nezan. 1979. "Kurdish Music and Dance." *The World of Music* 21:19–32.

Keyder, Çağlar. 1987. *State and Class in Turkey: A Study in Capitalist Development.* New York: Verso.

Kosnick, Kira. 2007. *Migrant Media: Turkish Broadcasting and Multicultural Politics in Berlin.* Bloomington: Indiana University Press.

Markoff, Irene. 2002. "Snapshot: Arif Sağ—Alevi *Bağlama* Teacher and Performer Par Excellence." In *Garland Encyclopedia of World Music, Volume 6: The Middle East*, ed. V. Danielson, S. Marcus, and D. Reynolds. New York: Routledge, 789–92.

O'Connell, John Morgan. 2000. "Fine Art, Fine Music: Controlling Turkish Taste at the Fine Arts Academy in 1926." *Yearbook for Traditional Music* 32:117–42.

Özer, Yetkin. 2003. "Crossing the Boundaries: The Akdeniz Scene and Mediterraneanness." In *Mediterranean Mosaic: Popular Music and Global Sounds*, ed. Geoffedo Plastino. New York: Routledge, 199–220.

Öztürkmen, Arzu. 1993. "Folklore and Nationalism in Turkey." Ph.D. Dissertation, University of Pennsylvania.

———. 2001. "Politics of National Dance in Turkey: A Historical Reappraisal." *Yearbook for Traditional Music* 33:139–43.

———. 2002. "'I Dance Folklore'." In *Fragments of Culture: The Everyday of Modern Turkey*, ed. D. Kandiyoti and A. Saktanber. London: I. B. Tauris & Co, 128–46

———. 2005. "Staging a Ritual Dance out of its Context: The Role of an Individual Artist in Transforming the Alevi *Semah.*" *Asian Folklore Studies* 64:247–60.

Sökefeld, Martin. 2008. *Struggling for Recognition: The Alevi Movement in Germany and in Transnational Space*. New York: Berghahn Books.

Stokes, Martin. 1994. "Place, Exchange and Meaning: Black Sea Musicians in the West of Ireland." In *Ethnicity, Identity and Music: The Musical Construction of Place*, ed. M. Stokes. Oxford: Berg, 97–115.

Tekelioğlu, Orhan. 2001. "Modernizing Reforms and Turkish Music in the 1930s." *Turkish Studies* 2(1):93–108.

Web Resources

www.kalan.com (record label specializing in urban and rural art and folk music and archival reissues)

www.neyzen.com (Klasik Türk Müziği notation and biography archive)

www.pankitap.com (primary publisher of research about music in Turkey; site in Turkish, but some books in English)

www.tulumba.com (North American importer of CDs and books released in Turkey)

www.turkishmusic.org (audio samples of numerous styles of music, and English-language articles on Turkish art music)

www.turkuler.com (database of *türkü* lyrics and notations, organized by region, title, and folklorist)

www.uskudarmusikicemiyeti.com/nota-arsivi.aspx (Üsküdar Müzik Cemiyeti archive of TSM and Klasik Türk Müziği notation)

Additional websites and print resources are located at www.oup.com/us/ globalmusic.

Index